Frederick E. Adair

The big Game of Baltistan and Ladakh

A summer in High Asia, being a record of sport and travel in Balistan and Ladakh

Frederick E. Adair

The big Game of Baltistan and Ladakh
A summer in High Asia, being a record of sport and travel in Balistan and Ladakh

ISBN/EAN: 9783744751636

Printed in Europe, USA, Canada, Australia, Japan

Cover: Foto ©Andreas Hilbeck / pixelio.de

More available books at **www.hansebooks.com**

The Big Game of Baltistan and Ladakh.

A SUMMER IN HIGH ASIA

BEING A RECORD OF SPORT
AND TRAVEL IN BALTISTAN
AND LADAKH

By CAPT. F. E. S. ADAIR
(LATE RIFLE BRIGADE)
AUTHOR OF "SPORT IN LADAKH"

WITH AN APPENDIX ON
CENTRAL ASIAN TRADE BY
CAPT. S. H. GODFREY.
(LATE BRITISH JOINT-COMMISSIONER AT LEH)

ILLUSTRATED FROM DRAWINGS BY
THE AUTHOR, PHOTOGRAPHS, AND
A MAP OF THE ROUTE.

LONDON: W. THACKER & CO.
2, CREED LANE, E.C.
CALCUTTA AND SIMLA : THACKER, SPINK & CO.
NEW YORK: 67, FIFTH AVENUE   1899

All rights reserved

CONTENTS.

CHAPTER I.

SRINAGAR—MATAIYAN.

Introductory, 1. The dilatory Asiatic, 2. Kashmir in April and May—Start from Srinagar, May 21, 1894—Ganderbal, 3. *Personnel* of the expedition, 4. The Sindh Valley, 7. Kangan—Caterpillar plague, 8. Two black bears seen at Goond—Gugangair—Sonamarg, 10. Red bear wounded near Baltal—Accident to Salia, 11. Watching an ibex-stalk, 12. The Zogi-La, 13. Ibex seen—Mitsahoï, 15. The Kashmiri marmot (*Arctomys Caudatus*), 16. Camp at Mataiyan—Difficulties of the route, 17. Three red bears seen near Pandras, 18. News of the Hushe Nalah, 19.

CHAPTER II.

MATAIYAN—HUSHE.

Scenery at Mataiyan and Dras, 20. The Dras Valley, 21. Bear seen by B., 22. Population of Dras—The Balti coolie, 23. Tashgaum—Ibex seen, 24. Rain—"'Dawai' not 'sharab,'" 25. B. and I part, 26. An afternoon scene, 27. Chanagand—Kirkichu, 28. Hardas—Scenery between Hardas and Olting-Thang—"Parris," 29. "Galleries," 30. Olting-Thang—Indus Valley, 31. The road, 33. "Jadoo"—Tarkutty—Ibex heads from the Hushe Nalah, 34. Kharmang—"Jhula" Bridge, 35. Story of a Khitmutgar—An ibex nalah, 37. An avalanche, 38. Tolti—Oriental etiquette, 39. Road to Parkutta, 40. Parkutta—The Shyok River and Valley, 41. Zāks, 42. Effect of "perwanas"—Kiris, 45. Kuru—Karku—A welcome note—A "drive," 46. Kapalu—Shale slopes—Machilu, 47. Masherbrum, 48. The Hushe River, 49. The Saltoro Valley, 50.

CONTENTS.

CHAPTER III.

HUSHE NALAH.

Blue rock-pigeons—Salia prospects, 51. Ibex and oorin (*Ovis vignei*) seen, 52. Oorin stalking—"Pulas," 53. "Stalking *my* oorin," 54. Another stalk, 55. Ibex seen—Kande—"Baksheesh," 56. Hushe Village—"W," 59. An amusing incident—Village and villagers of Hushe, 60. "Sahib Log," 61. Ibex-ravines, 62. Avalanches, 64. Ibex seen, 65. A stalk, 66. A "lucky expedition"—Ibex seen, 67. More ibex—Masherbrum by moonlight, 68. Sunrise on Masherbrum, 70. A lucky stalk, 72. *De gustibus non est disputandum*, 74. Newspapers, 75. Hushe—Kande—The unknown nalah, 76. Salia prospects—A fertile spot—Ibex seen, 78. Ibex again—A snow bridge—A stalk, 79. Kande, 80. Mountain sickness—Machilu—An interchange of courtesies—"Zāks," 81. A whirlwind—Abadon, 82.

CHAPTER IV.

KAPALU—LEH.

The Shyok Valley, 83. Do-oo—Kubaz, 84. Kustang—Marmots (*Arctomys aureus*)—Ram Chukore (*Tetraogallus Himalayensis*), 85. An unequalled panorama, 86. Thunder, wind, and rain—The Chorbat River, 88. "A lovely spot"—Golf, 89. A shooting competition—Saibra arrives, 90. News from B.—Marmots, 91. Concerning mountain sickness, 92. Crossing the Chorbat-La, 93. Entry into Ladakh, 94. "Perwanas" again—Goma Hanoo—Ibex seen, 97. A snow-leopard—A new bridge, 98. Floods at Yogma Hanoo—Babu Lal's butterfly-hunting, 99. "Mani" stones and "churtens," 100. Acheenathang—Garb of Ladakhi women, 101. "Mountains . . . gone mad," 102. Skirbichian—Doomkhar, 103. Story of Khalsi fort, 104. Utility of sporting trips—Khalsi, 106. Snurla—Munshi Palgez, 107. Saspul, 108. Bazgo—A prayer-wheel—Snemo, 109. Spitak—Leh, 110.

CHAPTER V.

LEH—GYA.

Leh, 111. The Gonpa—The Serai, 112. A varied diet, 113. The Wazir Wazarat—Ramzahn, 114. The Wazir's visit—The Indus again, 117. Chushot—Golab Bagh—Machalang, 118. The "Hemisphere," 119. Upshi—Horn-heaps, 120. Miru—Gya, 121. Scenery between Upshi and Gya, 122. Gya, 125.

CONTENTS.

CHAPTER VI.

GYA—KIAMERI-LA.

Gya Nalah—Kayma, 127. Tubbuh, 128. Nẏan (*Ovis Hodgsoni, Ovis Ammon*), 132. Nāpoo (*Ovis nahura*, Burhel), 135. Stalking nẏan, 139-142. Stalking nāpoo, 142-150. A wolf trap, 146. Crossing the Kiameri-La—Nẏan seen, 150.

CHAPTER VII.

RUPSHU.

Rupshu and its inhabitants (Chang-Pa), 152-162. Mountain sickness, 156. View from above Tiri Nalah—The Kyang (*Equus hemionus*), 162. *Lagomys Ladakensis*—A slough of despond, 165. Scenery round the Tso-Kar—In pursuit of a wolf, 166. Goa, kyang, and nẏan—A goa stalk, 169. Puttatuktuk and its goa, 170. An unsuccessful stalk, 171. Bower on goa—The Tso-Kar, 172. A nẏan stalk, 175. Goa stalking—The Polakonka Pass—Mountain sickness, 176. A nẏan stalk, 177. "H." of the Goorkhas, 178.

CHAPTER VIII.

POLAKONKA PASS—HANLÉ.

Puga—A search for goa, 179. Nāpoo seen—"Ee," 180. The Indus again—Camping ground near Nyuma Mud—Chinese Thibet, 181. Advice to sportsmen, 182. The Chagzōt, 186. "Chang," 187. Kyang seen—Mosquitoes, 188. A varied bag—Hanlé, 189. The Chagzōt's kindness—Chering Doorji, 191. "H." sets out for for the Koyul Nalah, 192. Kyang and nāpoo seen—Nẏan stalking, 193-200. A kyang stalk, 200. "H."'s sport in Koyul—A good spot for nāpoo, 201.

CHAPTER IX.

HANLÉ—GYA.

Goa ground—Kyang again—Goa stalking, 202-206. Poongook—Teal and duck shooting—Nāpoo seen—Crossing the Lanak-La, 209. *Vanessa Ladakensis*—Snipe seen at Dongan—Kyang—Goa stalking, 210. The Lam Tso, 211. A useful shelter—Goa seen—Ooti—sand-grouse, 212. Saibra sees a lynx—Lizards and locusts, 215. The Tso-Moriri, 216. Karzok—Shāpgo and Luglang Nalahs

CONTENTS.

—Peldo Le—Bar-headed geese, 217. An adventure—Polakonka Pass, 218. A peculiar phenomenon—Thugji—A shooting expedition, 221. Puttatuktuk—Pongonogo—Debring—The Tagalang Pass—A lammergeier shot—Gya again—Retrospect, 222.

CHAPTER X.

GYA—LEH.

Shāpoo ground—The Miru gorge, 224. And village—"Pudding stone"—Shāpoo stalking, 225-228. A "Shaitan" at Upshi, 228. "H." reappears at Machalang—Himis Gonpa, 231-234. Golab-Bagh—Chushot—Leh—The Bazaar, 234.

CHAPTER XI.

LEH—SRINAGAR—HOME.

Snemo—Saspul—Bazgo, 236. Snurla—A good performance—Incident at Khalsi, 237. "A magnificent sight," 238. Lamayuru, 241. The Fotu Pass—Kharbu—The Namika Pass—Wakha—Moulbekh, 242. Visit from Munshi Palgez—Shergol—Farewell to Ladakh, 243. Pushkim—"H." and "W." arrive—Baltistan once more, 244. Chanagand — Skardo — Tashgaum — Dras, 245. Mataiyan Valley—Kashmiri marmot shot, 246. On the Zogi-La—Strange accident to a pony, 249. The barasingh—Srinagar, October 18, 250. Rawal Pindi—Bombay—Home, 251.

APPENDIX.

THE TRADE OF LADAKH WITH CHINA AND THIBET.

By Capt. S. H. Godfrey (late British Joint Commissioner at Leh), 255.

LIST OF BUTTERFLIES FROM THIBET, 281, 282.

LIST OF ILLUSTRATIONS.

	PAGE
PORTRAIT OF AUTHOR WITH SHIKARIS AND TROPHIES *Frontispiece*	
Kashmiri primulas	1
LOOKING UP THE SINDH VALLEY FROM SONAMARG, KASHMIR	8
AT THE FOOT OF THE ZOGI-LA RAVINE, NEAR BALTAL	11
LOOKING BACK DOWN THE SINDH VALLEY (KASHMIR) FROM BALTAL	12
CROSSING THE ZOGI-LA	14
THE ZOGI-LA	15
LADAKHI WOMAN AND CHILD	19
Kashmiri Iris	20
A BALTI COOLIE	23
BALTI ROADWAY	32
A CORNER ON THE INDUS ROAD	33
"JHULA" BRIDGE AT KHARTAKSHO	35
JHULA BRIDGE OVER RIVER INDUS	36
INDUS ROAD, "BETWEEN KHARMANG AND TOLTI"	38
CROSSING THE SHYOK RIVER ON ZĀKS (SKIN RAFTS)	43
LOOKING UP THE HUSHE NALAH	49
MARMOT	50
SHYOK VALLEY FROM MACHILU	51
IBEX GROUND	52
VILLAGE IN THE HUSHE NALAH—DOLOMITE PEAKS	57
SIDE NALAH OFF THE HUSHE VALLEY	64
SUNRISE ON MASHERBRUM	70
"THE OLD BUCKS APPEARED"	72
"I RAISED MY RIFLE AND FIRED AT THE BIG ONE"	73
VIEW IN SIDE NALAH OFF THE HUSHE VALLEY	77
"WE CAMPED IN THE MIDDLE OF QUITE A WOOD"	78
A SNOW BRIDGE	79
WILD COLUMBINE (BALTISTAN)	83
CAMP BELOW CHORBAT-LA (STORMY WEATHER ON THE GLACIER)	89
CROSSING THE CHORBAT-LA (17,000 FEET) FROM BALTISTAN INTO LADAKH	95

LIST OF ILLUSTRATIONS.

	PAGE
"At last a new bridge was completed"	98
On the Road to Leh, Village of Saspul	108
Ruined Buddhist Village of Bazgo	109
"Mani" Stone	110
The Central Asian Road leading into Leh	115
Looking up the Indus Valley from Machalang	119
The Town of Leh	123
Camp in the Gya Nalah	128
Leh	129
Leh	137
The British Joint-Commissioner's House at Leh	143
"We clambered down... and peeped over"	148
Group of Yāks, Leh	153
The Cornfields of Leh	159
"We came upon a very striking scene"	166
Churten in the City of Leh	167
Camp at the Tso-Kar—Yāks Feeding	172
The State Dispensary in Leh	173
Anemometer and Meteorological Station at Leh	183
Indus Valley at Nyuma Mud	185
Fortified Monastery of Hanlé	190
Himis Monastery	207
"This lake is surrounded by yellow and red hills"	213
Sunset on the Tso-Moriri	216
The Chagzōt and Lamas of the Himis Monastery	219
Churtens and Mani on the Road below Himis	229
Young Buddhist Red Lama	232
Buddhist silver and copper shrine box, and metal opium pipe	235
"H." and the Author, with their Ladakh Trophies	236
On the Srinagar-Leh Road: Monastery and Village of Lamayuru	239
On the Road to Leh: Village and Monastery of Chamba-Moulbekh	241
Rdungsten in the Himis Monastery	247
Buddhist Prayer-wheel	251
Sooroo Bridge, under construction	269
„ „ completed	273
Curios from Leh	277

INTRODUCTION.

I FEEL bound, in submitting this book to the public, to explain that it is nothing more than the diary of a journey, undertaken in the summer of 1894, in pursuit of pleasure and the big game of Baltistan and Ladakh. I know that it is without any literary pretension whatever, being merely an account of an expedition such as is undertaken by many travellers and sportsmen every year, and cannot pretend to any geographical or other discoveries.

The heights of mountains, etc., are copied from the Government Survey; the heads of the trophies measured and recorded by Rowland Ward, and the collection of Lepidoptera classified at the Natural History Museum, South Kensington. My best thanks are due to Captain Godfrey (late Joint-Commissioner of Ladakh), not only for his kindness in assisting my expedition, but also for the chapter on Central Asian trade at the end of the book; he also was most kind in revising proofs, and supplying some of the beautiful photographs taken by himself at and near Leh, etc. My thanks are also due to

INTRODUCTION.

Mr. H. Lindsay (late Gordon Highlanders) for the excellent photographs of Baltistan.

I may say that my only hope in setting forth the diary of a successful expedition is that it may be of some interest and use to other sportsmen intending to follow in the same track; and may they enjoy themselves as much, and have as good luck, as befell the Author during his "Summer in High Asia."

London, 1899.   F. E. S. ADAIR.

A SUMMER IN HIGH ASIA.

CHAPTER I.

Kashmiri primulas.

WHERE is the traveller who, having gazed on a mighty range of hills in an unknown land, has not experienced a kind of fascination and indefinite longing to surmount the barrier and see, with his own eyes, what lies beyond? It was with such a feeling that I had gazed on the Himalaya from the Indian side when prevented by a soldier's duties and a want of time from crossing their snows to explore the regions on the farther slopes; and I had looked with envy on those more fortunate individuals who brought back tales of the wonderful countries and "Sportsman's Paradises" which might be reached if leisure permitted. Accordingly, it was with feelings of more than pleasurable anticipation that I found myself gazing once more on the hills that surround the lovely vale of Kashmir, and felt that time was now no object, and that I was free to wander over them as fancy, or the chances of sport might dictate. It is, however, as every traveller in the East well knows, one thing to propose to start on an expedition forthwith, and quite another to find oneself *en route*. Even with the best laid schemes, and every preparation carefully made beforehand, one is apt to find oneself defeated by the dilatory Asiatic, and patience is a virtue that should certainly be cultivated by a traveller in the East. I was not fortunate in starting on the expedition that is here to be narrated, and the unforeseen delays seemed so interminable that at last I began to wonder if I should ever get off at all. My stores, which were of necessity somewhat considerable, as I had not made up my mind as to where I was going, or for how long I should be away, failed to turn up from Bombay, though I knew that they were on the road somewhere between Rawal Pindi and Srinagar. To storm at the carrying company who had undertaken to convey them was useless; the more angry I became, the more the native clerk would smile, promise, and relapse into Oriental indifference; nor was it until I had enlisted the kind offices of a R.E. officer, who was in charge of the road, and who ultimately discovered them, forgotten at some wayside station, and had them sent on post-haste, that I managed to retrieve them. However, one might spend one's time worse than by passing the months of April and May in Kashmir, which surely at this time of year must be hard to beat anywhere for beauty. The trees, meadows, and even houses, are covered with many-coloured flowers, while the whiteness of the snows, still low down on the mountain-sides, forms a brilliant background to every picturesque scene. Nor had I eventually any cause to regret the delay, though I have mentioned it here to explain the lateness of my departure (so late was it, indeed, that everyone declared that I might as well give up the expedition as far as sport was concerned), since, during my stay in Srinagar, I formed the acquaintance of many kind friends, amongst them the Joint-Commissioner of Ladakh, Captain S. H. Godfrey, to whom I was subsequently so much indebted for the success of my expedition. The pleasures of a sojourn in the beautiful Vale of Kashmir have been so often dilated upon by abler pens that it is unnecessary for me to add anything here; so suffice it to say, that after a pleasant stay, during which I spent some time in pursuing apocryphal black bears, and getting into training on the steep hillsides that surround the Woolar Lake, I eventually set forth from Srinagar on the 21st of May, 1894, and reached the first stage, the village of Ganderbal, that evening.

A SUMMER IN HIGH ASIA.

It was 6.30 A.M. on the 22nd of May before I left Ganderbal and started on my expedition to the higher regions. Perhaps, before going farther, it will be well for me to introduce the chief individuals of the *personnel* of my expedition who accompanied me without change throughout my journey. First, and most important, was my Hindu bearer, by name Babu Lal. He had been retained for me, before I arrived in India, by an old brother officer who was at that time serving on the Viceroy's staff. To me Babu Lal was invaluable. Having twice been on active service as an officer's servant in mountain campaigns, he had acquired a knowledge of camp life that made a considerable difference to my comfort. A good mountaineer, he was always willing and hard-working; and I really believe that he took as much interest in his master's sport as did "the sahib" himself. Never was any work too hard for him. After a long and weary march there he was to be seen, washing clothes, mending them, or doing something equally useful, as cheerfully as if he had been in camp all day. He alone of my camp spoke a few words of English. The head of the sporting department was my shikari, Salia Lohn, well known to many sportsmen who have shot in Kashmir. He also had been retained for me some months beforehand, by the aforesaid friend at Simla, as being generally acknowledged to be one of the best shikaris in Kashmir. A square-built, active man, rather beyond the middle age, with an intelligent face deeply pitted with small-pox, the best recommendation that I can give him is that on no single occasion during the five months that I was shooting did he fail to bring me within firing distance of the game that we were stalking. When it is taken into consideration that most of these stalks were undertaken on the open hillsides of Ladakh the record is a truly marvellous, and, I should think, unequalled one.

Of course we were greatly favoured by luck, but he seemed to have a real knowledge of the habits of the animals, and his patience was extraordinary; but what struck me most, knowing the habits of the genus shikari, was that instead of urging me to fire at any animal within range, however small his head, so that he might subsequently boast of the number of so and so that his "sahib" had shot, he would frequently say, even when after a laborious stalk we had at length got within range, "Sahib, there is no animal with a head worth keeping; leave them to grow bigger." Sportsmen who have been in Kashmir will appreciate this. He was always telling me that his father and grandfather had been professional shikaris before him, I suppose with a view of impressing upon me that he had been brought up "in the trade." In manner he was rather independent, but after I had once or twice shown him that I meant to do what *I* wanted and not what *he* wanted, was quite willing to do his best. As second shikari I took Salia's eldest son Saibra. Every whit as keen, though perhaps not quite so experienced as his father, Saibra was one of the pleasantest natives with whom I have ever had to deal. He had been educated by a "Moulvie," who seems to have acted as a sort of private tutor. Saibra could read and write Persian fluently, which sometimes proved of great use. He had most cultivated and refined ideas for a native, and was, as far as I saw, quite trustworthy (most wonderful for a Kashmiri!). When I started after ibex in Baltistan I lent Saibra to a friend of mine, B., who was going to shoot for some three weeks in Kashmir, with instructions that, after B.'s trip was over, he was to take charge of the provisions, &c., that I was sending direct to Leh, and was to meet me there. B. afterwards wrote and told me that he was more than satisfied with Saibra. My "chota" shikari was Ullia, a bright and intelligent Kashmiri, a wonderful mountaineer to whom I am indebted for the head of more than one animal that got away wounded and that he recovered from an apparently inaccessible place. His eyesight was marvellous, even for a "Pahari," and he was always willing to help about the camp and to do any odd job that was wanted. When I have mentioned "Sekour Khan," my Mussulman "khitmutgar" and cook, always grave, sometimes frightened, but accepting everything with the calmness engendered by a belief that it was "Kismet" and couldn't be helped, and who always rose to the occasion and cooked a good dinner (indeed, very often the greater the apparent difficulties the better the repast), I think that I have described the chiefs of each department. Of course, besides these there were some permanent coolies who were always with me, and who were employed in carrying my food when I was shooting, in fetching water, taking heads down to Kashmir, fetching my mails, and other odd jobs.

The beauties of the Sindh Valley have been so often described in detail that it would be superfluous to do so here. The main road from India to Leh, and indeed to Central Asia, runs through its lovely scenery. Fertile and well-cultivated fields surrounding pleasant villages whose timber-built homesteads, nestling beneath their shady walnut-trees, remind one of Swiss farm-houses (in fact, all the scenery here is like that of some of the more picturesque valleys of Switzerland), alternate with wilder gorges and flowering jungles on either side of the River Sindh. Above them rise steep grassy slopes and pine-clad spurs leading up to the lofty buttresses and precipices of the Sacred Haramook and other mountains, while above these again are the shining snows and the glittering glaciers of the higher hills. After passing Sonamarg the scenery becomes more exclusively Alpine; the open "Margs" or Alps, bright with wild flowers, rising gradually till Baltal is reached; a collection of small huts at the foot of the Zogi-La (11,500 feet) by

A SUMMER IN HIGH ASIA.

LOOKING UP THE SINDH VALLEY FROM SONAMARG, KASHMIR.

which pass the road leads over the main range into Baltistan. To return to my journey. Leaving Ganderbal we crossed the "Karewah" or elevated plateau, at this time bright with the blossoms of wild roses of every tint from crimson to white, and following a path that led downhill through thick jungle, we crossed the river and arrived at Kangan (12 miles), a pleasant camping-ground. During this march I was glad to bid farewell to a hairy caterpillar which they told me had become a plague in Kashmir during the last three years. I had been surprised when exploring some of the lower jungles, to find that my shikaris warned me not to pitch my tent under certain trees, especially willows, also to tie a handkerchief round my neck, and in fact to cover all bare skin when passing through particular tracts of jungle; but I was soon to be taught the cause of this solicitude by an object lesson. Having one day neglected their cautions and brushed against a bush in one of these tracts with my bare wrist, I presently felt a tingling sensation which, on my rubbing the place, seemed to grow worse, and on return to camp became inflamed and swollen; I did not recover from this for ten days or a fortnight, and afterwards did as I was told! I found out afterwards that the trees and jungle were in some places almost stripped of leaves, and were covered with what looked like spider-webs, but which were in reality nests of small hairy caterpillars rather like those of our Currant-moth (*Abraxas grossulariata*). It appears that these on contact leave their hairs in one's skin with the afore-mentioned irritating effect. When "stung" the natives scrub the place with earth or sand, which may remove the hairs; but rubbing with the hand seems to have the effect of sending them into the skin with the unpleasant result described. I was not sorry to hear that these pests did not exist beyond Kangan. The natives told me that until some three years previously, they had been unknown, and I should think that they are praying for their speedy departure.

From Kangan the next march was to Goond

(fourteen miles). Here, while I was resting in my tent about sunset, my shikaris came to tell me that there were two black bears on the opposite side of the river. I rushed out with my rifle just as I was, in dressing-gown and slippers, but the bears were disappearing into the jungle. I could not in any case have crossed the river, and was not particularly sorry that they had escaped, as I had shot many before, and at this time of year their coats are not at their best.

However, hearing from B. that he was coming up to join me and was encamped some eight miles lower down, and knowing that he had never had any hill shooting, I wrote to him advising him to try the opposite side of the river on the following morning, on the chance of seeing the bears, and telling him to meet me at the next stage, Gugangair. This he did, but though he found their tracks he could not find the bears, as the jungle was thick. Together B. and I marched from Gugangair up the magnificent ravine through which the road leads to Sonamarg. Here the Sindh river forces its way between tremendous precipices over a rocky bed. The couloirs were still full of snow, and in one place Salia carried me on his back for some distance, up to his knees in the stream and stooping low under the cornice formed by the end of a snow-slope. From beautiful Sonamarg, a broad Alp bright with yellow crocus (from which it is said to take its name "Golden Meadow") we

A SUMMER IN HIGH ASIA.

marched to Baltal (ten miles), the aforesaid group of huts at the foot of the Zogi Pass. Salia said that here, though it is so accessible from Srinagar, ibex might often be seen, or at any rate red bear, in a valley that runs to the east, towards the sacred caves of Amarnath, so we decided to halt for a day while B. pursued them. The evening of the day we arrived he wounded, but did not get, a red bear. Whilst following its tracks the next morning he lost the bear and I very nearly lost my shikari! It appears that the party were crossing a steep snow-slope, cutting steps as they went, when Salia missed his footing and started off down the incline. Unable to stop himself he went faster and faster and just as it seemed that he must inevitably be dashed to pieces on the rocks below, was providentially stopped by a birch tree which was projecting above the snow. (When an accident of this sort occurs to a sure-footed native, one cannot help thinking that it might easily happen

AT THE FOOT OF THE ZOGI-LA RAVINE, NEAR BALTAL.

A SUMMER IN HIGH ASIA.

to oneself.) For a time he was quite unnerved, and could do nothing. During the afternoon of this day I had the somewhat unusual experience of watching somebody else stalking an ibex, which proved almost as exciting as stalking oneself, as both quarry and pursuer were in sight for some hours through the glasses. However on

LOOKING BACK DOWN THE SINDH VALLEY (KASHMIR) FROM BALTAL.

this occasion the ground was impracticable and the goats escaped; but it was interesting to watch the latter, unconscious that they were being pursued, slowly crossing what appeared to be a perpendicular face of rock certainly 2,000 feet from crest to base. The following morning we

A SUMMER IN HIGH ASIA.

were to cross the Zogi-La, the pass through the only real depression that occurs in the main range for many hundreds of miles on either side. The pass is not a high one (some 11,500 feet), but it has a bad name, chiefly, I think, because of the sudden high winds which, accompanied by freezing snow-storms, come sweeping along the main range, and are carried through this funnel, as it were, into the country beyond. Usually after the month of May (the date, however, depends on the snow-fall of the previous winter), the path winds up the hill on the N.W. side of the ravine till it reaches the summit of the pass, some 2,000 feet above the huts at Baltal, but till then, the slopes being covered with snow and very steep, the road lies up the bed of the chasm, which makes it fairly hard work to cross, as the ice and snow, filling the ravine, present a series of steep ascents to get up which steps have to be cut. When we arrived the summer path up the slopes was not yet feasible, though uncovered in places, but the way up the nalah had been pretty well trodden by the many travellers who had already crossed. It was nearly five o'clock on the following morning before we were off, but as the sun does not reach the snow on the Kashmir side till it has been up some time, it is not so important to make an early start here as is the case on some passes. At first our way lay up the frozen ice-slopes in the bottom of the ravine and it was pretty stiff going, but after climbing for some two or three miles we came out upon undulating snow-fields. The last birch-trees were now left behind, and we had bidden farewell to fertility, at any rate to wild fertility, for many a month to come. The summit of the pass was a wilderness of snow with rocky peaks on either side, and so level that it was impossible to tell where the watershed might be,

CROSSING THE ZOGI-LA.

the only break in the white monotony being the tops of the telegraph-poles, a sign of civilization which accompanies the traveller as far as Kargil, on the Leh, and Skardo on the Baltistan, roads. By the time that the sun, rising over the eastern hills, shone on the snow that had fallen freshly during

A SUMMER IN HIGH ASIA.

the night, we were glad that we had taken the usual precautions of covering our faces with vaseline and putting on tinted spectacles, as the glare was very trying. At the summit of the pass some diversion was caused by the sight of a herd of ibex on the rocks above, but these turned out to be all females and young bucks. About nine o'clock we

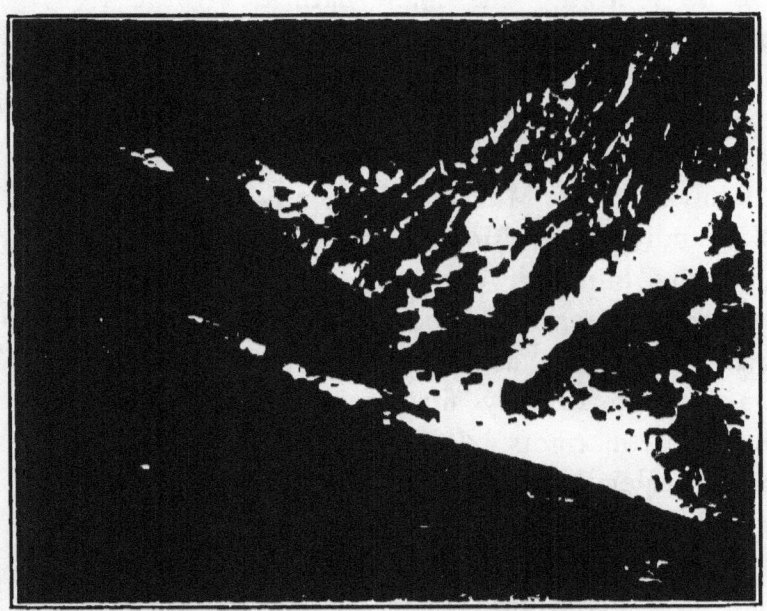

THE ZOGI-LA.

reached the huts of Mitsahoï which are built here as a shelter for the dâk runners. One of these hovels was closed with a Purdah, and we heard that a young coolie had been born there on the previous day (fancy alluding to one's birthplace as a stone hut on the summit of the Zogi-La). Not long afterwards the snow began to disclose patches of rock and earth as we descended towards the next stage, Mataiyan. The descent on the Baltistan side is so gradual, that were it not for the fact that the stream flows to the E. instead of the W., you would scarcely observe for some distance that you were going downhill. Soon after this I parted from B., he following the main path down the right bank of the stream that eventually becomes the Dras River, whilst I went down the left bank on the chance of seeing a red bear, which Salia said were sometimes to be found on the slopes opposite Mataiyan. At Mitsahoï I found a sturdy little Yarkandi pony waiting for me, and was not sorry to mount him after our walk over the snow, which towards the end had become somewhat toilsome owing to the sun having made it soft. Soon afterwards I made my first acquaintance with the Kashmiri marmots (*Arctomys Caudatus*), which are much larger than their Alpine congeners and are of a reddish-brown colour. On seeing us approach they sat up, generally on a stone, whistling shrilly, and soon dived into their burrows. I found out subsequently that though one can get easily to within even gun-shot of them, unless they are dropped dead on the spot, they almost invariably get away into their earths, and that to bag them the most effectual weapon is a rook-rifle. After following the stream for some distance, we came to some very steep "couloirs" filled with snow, which ran down to the stream from the precipices above. I thought these slopes quite steep enough for ourselves to cross, and was fairly astonished to see the pony, left to his own devices, calmly following us, picking his way along the footsteps that we had made.

Not long afterwards we arrived opposite Mataiyan, where we could see that our camp had been already pitched, but between us and it was a great gulf fixed, in the shape of the Dras stream, by this time a very respectable torrent. However, by dint of hailing at the top of our voices, we managed to attract the attention of a man with a drove of ponies on the opposite side, and told him that we wanted to cross. He shook his head, but being persuaded by our somewhat vehement gesticulations, he tried to drive some of his ponies over the stream in order to ascertain its depth; they, however, declined to be so driven. At last, in desperation, my Yarkandi pony was induced to enter the torrent, and struggled bravely across; so we called out to our friends on the opposite side to send him back to take us over, intending to cross one by one on his back. But here an unexpected difficulty awaited us; he had gone over willingly enough, but nothing would induce him to return, and he finally galloped off gaily to the camp, which he, as well as ourselves, had noticed. After spending some little time in disappointment (not silent), we realised that there was nothing for it but to go down stream some four miles to Pandras, where there is a bridge, and then return a like distance up the opposite side of the stream to the camp. This was rather trying, as we were not more than half a mile in a straight line from the latter, and had already been going for some twelve hours. But the greatest difficulty was still to come. About a mile further on the ground was cut away by a landslip, which fell almost perpendicularly into the torrent below; it was only about 100 yards across, and to go round and above it would have entailed climbing some thousands of feet to the top of the range, so we determined to cross the face. To do this we had to cut steps and to rope ourselves together with turbans, and I, for one, was not sorry when we reached the opposite side in safety; the fact that the river was boiling along some fifty feet below not adding to one's sensations of pleasure. After this we went along some ground at the foot of slopes which looked made for red bear, but there were none to be seen, and we eventually reached the bridge at Pandras, where we were glad to find ponies (the recalcitrant Yarkandi amongst them) awaiting us. We trotted gaily back the other side of the river towards camp. After going about a mile, Salia said, "Look!" and on my looking, there were three red bears calmly feeding on the very slopes under which we had passed only an hour before! We arrived in camp about 8 P.M., having had about fifteen hours' pretty hard work. I found that an officer of the R.H.A. was also camping here. He had been early in Baltistan, and had obtained very good sport in a nalah called Hushe, where, in spite of bad weather, he had bagged several fine ibex. He said that he had been succeeded in the valley by a friend of mine, W., so I determined to make this nalah my goal, as W. would probably be leaving just about the time that I should arrive there. Salia thought that I could not do better, but at the same time he told me, as everybody else had done, that it was too late in the season for me to expect any sport with the ibex, as they would have gone so high, as the snow melted, that it would be difficult to find them; in fact, the coolie-loads of ibex horns going down to Srinagar that we met on the road, showed me that most men were returning just as I was setting out. However, I determined that to the Hushe nalah I would go, and my hitherto undecided wanderings had henceforward a definite objective.

LADAKHI WOMAN AND CHILD.

CHAPTER II.

Kashmiri Iris.

THERE are few views more striking, even among the wonderful scenes in the Himalaya, than the valley in which Mataiyan is situated, as seen when you are coming from Kashmir. In the first place, you have entered quite a new country as soon as you have crossed the Zogi Pass. The smiling landscapes of Kashmir have been left behind, with their pine-clad slopes and fertile valleys, and you see before you a wilderness of desolate hillsides and stony wastes. The reason is, of course, that the rain-charged clouds brought up by the monsoon winds are stopped by the barrier of the Main Range, and it is curious to observe how, within a few miles of the Pass, the vegetation decreases and gradually ceases, so that by the time that you arrive at Dras,.the next camping-ground after Mataiyan, you are in the midst of true Thibetan scenery—rocky precipices and pinnacles, with slopes and "talus" of stone and shale and alluvial "fans," where the only spots of fertility are the terraced fields of the scattered villages, which are always situated at the mouth of some side valley, where the water of the mountain torrent that comes down the ravine can be used for the purposes of artificial irrigation. But here it is not this sudden change alone from wooded hillsides to barren mountains that strikes the traveller; just beyond the huts of Mataiyan is a group of some of the most magnificent precipices that I have ever seen, which rise up almost sheer for some thousands of feet from the valley to a collection of rocky peaks. This mountain is known to the natives as being the home of the resident "Deva," or guardian spirit of Baltistan, of whom more anon. These crags were rendered more than ever imposing at the time when we were there by the tremendous avalanches which came pouring over them, and which, starting with a noise like thunder, long before they reached the valley had become impalpable dust, like a glorified Staubbach.

The level bottom of the valley through which the Dras River wanders was now a golden carpet of crocuses, and the peaks on the west side, where I had seen the bears, were of the ordinary type of rocky precipice and slope. The following day B., being unable to cross the river where I had been stopped the day before, was off early in pursuit of the bears, and had to go down to the Pandras Bridge and ascend the left bank. I watched him for some time through the glasses as he scaled the snow-slopes and precipices, and then rode on my way. Soon the gorge narrowed, and in one place it looked as if one might almost have jumped across the chasm through which the river flowed between the huge rocks. These rocks were quite smooth, and looked polished and of a deep brown colour, owing to the action of the atmosphere. This outer coat can be easily scraped away, showing a light colour below, a fact which is curiously apparent in places where the passers-by have scratched rude figures of ibex with colossal horns, quaint-looking figures, and rough inscriptions upon them. While I was eating my lunch B. joined me, having seen a bear, but been unable to get a shot. Some few miles farther on we suddenly emerged from the ravine into the Dras Valley. Here the scenery is almost like that of Ladakh, the level plain being surrounded by hills with rounded tops, whose slopes, composed of shale and loose boulders, are striped with every shade of ochre and red, and even of light blue and yellow. The valley itself is considered fertile in these parts, and there are many cultivated fields and pastures of scanty grass. A prominent feature is the small fort, looking like some toy fortress, which is built quite low down so as to be easily commanded by the heights on every side; scarcely our idea of a good position, but perhaps the situation is rendered necessary for purposes of a water supply, and is good enough against the attacks of the enemy whom it was constructed to withstand.

Crossing a rickety cantilever bridge, from which an Englishman, we were told, had fallen and been drowned some few years back, we galloped on to the camping-ground, which is an enclosure with a few unhappy-looking poplars, the only trees in the valley, planted round it, just in time to escape a terrific hail-storm.

A BALTI COOLIE.

The population of Dras is a mixed one, consisting of Baltis, a few Ladakis, Dards, and a sect known as Brōkpa. Here we changed our Kashmiri coolies, who had come from Goond, for Baltis. The Balti coolie is a curious-looking being. He shaves the back of his head, the hair escaping from his little rolled-up cap in long ringlets that hang on either side over his ears; it seems marvellous how his garments, consisting of a coarsely-woven tunic and pyjamas, can hold together, so ragged are they, whilst his legs and feet are clad in boots, of which the upper part is composed of rough skins and the sole of bundles of rags, with a view to protecting his feet from the terrible sharp stones and boulders of which the roads in his country are composed. Every Balti coolie carries a needle and thread to sew these rags together when occasion demands, and it is by no means an uncommon sight to see him sitting down by the roadside repairing his foot gear. A quiet, uncomplaining creature, there is something almost pathetic about the Balti, though in some districts, for instance, high up the Shyok River, and in places where they are less used to being suddenly impressed to carry travellers' baggage or for Government "begar" (forced labour), they are far more independent in manner. I found them on the whole a cheery and inoffensive people. Every coolie carries a stick, in shape somewhat resembling a wooden pickaxe, and on this when tired he rests his load, as the exertion of getting up again if he once sat down would be too wearisome.

The following day we traversed the Dras valley, riding for some miles along the open plain, where the vivid green of the young grass contrasted strangely with the brilliant colours of the foot-hills and the purple canopy of rain-cloud that concealed the higher peaks. Our way led down a narrow gorge above the river, and we arrived in a storm of rain at Tashgaum (fifteen miles). The only objects of interest seen during this march were a herd of female ibex high up amongst the crags near the latter place, and a weary pedestrian with fair complexion and beard, whom B. declared was a Russian spy, and whom we passed and repassed. On our questioning him he merely remarked the word "Yarkand," and from what I saw subsequently I imagine that he was a harmless Central Asian returning to his native land. At Tashgaum we

A SUMMER IN HIGH ASIA.

found a most sporting officer who had come from Aden in quest of ibex, but though he had seen some here that had good heads, he had not yet had a shot. Throughout the night of May 30th the rain poured upon us in deluges, soaking the outer fly of our tents, and turning the camping-ground into a quagmire. On this, and subsequent occasions of extreme wet and cold, I served out some rum and hot water to the servants who had accompanied me from the plains of India, and made them drink it in my presence. I overcame the scruples of my Mussulman khitmutgar by telling him that it was "dawai," or medicine, and not "sharab," or intoxicating liquor, which of course no good Mohammedan would touch! This rum was given to prevent them getting a chill, which at once knocks over an Indian servant, and thereby renders him not only useless, but a drag upon his master's movements, as the wretched man cannot be left to his own devices when ill and in a strange land. I have over and over again heard of a promising expedition having been spoilt by an Indian servant having fallen ill, so that the simple prescription of rum and hot water administered as a preventive is one worth remembering.

By the following morning the rain had ceased, though the higher hills were still veiled in misty vapour. We had to delay our start until our tents were dry enough to be carried (wet as they were their weight was increased four-fold), so that we did not get away till 10 o'clock, rather a late hour, especially as I had a twenty-mile march before me. At the bridge, about one mile below Tashgaum, B. and I parted, he going down the left bank of the stream by a goat-path, on his way to the Shingo nalah, whilst I followed the main road to Leh down the right bank. For some miles we kept abreast, and could almost have shouted to one another across the torrent; but some way farther down the gorge my way led over a steep spur, while his path led round some rocks just above the water's edge, and the last view I had of B. was seeing him spread-eagled and sticking like a fly to a window pane, on a perpendicular-faced rock just above the foaming torrent, while Saibra, who was like a cat on this sort of ground, was helping him over. One of B.'s coolies fell into the stream at this point, but he and his load were fortunately rescued. My way now became dreary in the extreme, more particularly as I was without my cheery companion. Up and down we went along the stony and desolate gorge as I then thought it, though on the return journey it seemed all that was beautiful and fertile; rocky crags shut out the view on either side, and here and there we had to cross a snow-slope. On one of these latter a pony, the one carrying my tent, lost his footing and very nearly disappeared for ever, which would have been inconvenient. Soon after this I met my first Ladaki, with his flat, cheerful, Mongolian face and queer little pigtail. He was driving a zho, a sort of compromise between the yāk and ordinary bullock.

In the afternoon the sun came out, and the whole scene became imbued with a colouring that was strange to me; the lower crags were brilliant with every imaginable shade of purple, yellow, and red; above them shone the pure white of the freshly-fallen snow against a bright blue sky, whilst violet shadows were reflected on the vivid blue-green of the torrent, a picture which to be appreciated must be seen. The vegetation had now become scanty, a few willows and cypress bushes by the stream, with wild roses that were at this elevation not yet in bloom, and wild currant bushes (*Ribes ladakensis*). On the stony slopes were a few aromatic shrubs, prominent amongst them the "Boortse" (*Eurotia*), with which I was destined to become so well acquainted subsequently, and wild lavender. Among the rocks above flourished the pencil cedar (*Juniperus excelsa*), which grows singly wherever the roots can cling to the steep and stony hillside, and which gives the mountains a curiously spotted appearance. During this part of the march a huge rock, whose weather-worn surface of a deep brown that was scrawled over with the rough figures of ibex, was a very prominent object, and a friend of mine who had marched along the road some two months previously, told me that at that time this rock was the only feature in an otherwise unbroken expanse of snow. About 5 P.M. we reached the small village of Chanagand, and here we were to leave the main road to Leh and follow the Dras River to its junction with the Indus. On the opposite side was Kirkichu, the fertility of whose terraced fields, at this time green with sprouting corn, was a welcome relief after the glare of the stony wastes along which we had been travelling all day. A sharp descent led us down to the rickety bridge by which the river is crossed, and the path, already very different to the main road which we had just left, led up the side of a steep hill. One of the first features of a view in Baltistan that strikes the traveller is a green streak that is generally to be seen near any village, running almost horizontally along the barren face of the mountain, often crossing apparently inaccessible precipices; this is, in fact, the little irrigation channel that, starting far up in some mountain ravine, brings down the water to which the village owes its fertility, and in fact, its existence; the vivid green is produced by the herbage and even little shrubs which spring up on these apparently sterile places if only there is a constant supply of water. There is one of these ducts high up on the precipice above Kirkichu, and on the occasion of our passing a breach had been made in this channel, and the water, pouring down the almost perpendicular face, had struck the path, and flowing down it for a short distance, had almost washed it away. However, we struggled through, almost up to our knees in mud, and keeping a sharp

A SUMMER IN HIGH ASIA.

look-out for the cannonade of stones that came rattling down from above.*

After a somewhat toilsome progression along the narrow path, we reached the village of Hardas, where we were to halt, just as it was getting dark. What attracted my attention here was the road to Leh, winding along the apparently vertical precipice, and along which I was destined to wend my homeward way some five months later. The following day our march took us to a village called "Olting-Thang" (seventeen miles), and I think that perhaps of all the dull marches on the Dras and Skardo road this is the dullest, as well as one of the most arduous. For a few miles you follow the Dras River till you arrive at the point where it is joined by the stream from Sooroo which comes in from the E. Near here I saw some disused pits which the natives said had been dug to find gems (probably sapphires). At this point you enter a gorge running N.W., bounded on either side by granite rocks. The road henceforward leads either over steep slopes of stones that have fallen from the crags above, and which vary in size from a pebble to a railway-carriage, or else you are climbing over precipitous ridges ("parris," as they are locally termed), some thousands of feet high and falling sheer to the river. These are usually crossed by

* It was whilst photographing this watercourse from the opposite side that Knight's camera came to grief.—"Where Three Empires Meet," Chap. VIII.

means of "galleries," that is to say, a sort of staircase of flagstones, and by no means stable ones at that, is conducted along the face of the precipices, supported on rough beams, which in their turn are held up by stakes stuck into any crevice in the rock that may be handy. Journeying along a road of this sort, with a June sun full on one's back at midday, and with the glare from the surrounding rocks as bad as the rays of the sun itself, is the sort of thing that makes one ask oneself if it is good enough to undergo all this on the off chance of getting a shot at a buck goat! However, all one's ills are forgotten as soon as one arrives at a village, and one can truly appreciate the feelings of a traveller in the desert who at last reaches an oasis. These villages, as already described, are invariably situated at the mouth of a side ravine and are irrigated by a stream from above. Their terraced fields, to make which the earth is carried up in baskets from the torrent-bed below, were, at the time that we saw them, brilliant with the green of the young corn, and shaded with the bright tints of the apricot trees, contrasting with the bluer hues of the poplars and willows. Every field was bordered with wild roses and lilac-coloured dwarf iris, while innumerable magpies and golden orioles added animation to the scene. The villages themselves are composed of little square boxes of huts with walls of mud, wedged tightly together and hopelessly dirty; but the population, at least the male portion of it, seem a fairly healthy and cheery lot. The females fly into their houses at the approach of a stranger, or, if in the cornfields, throw themselves on the ground and lie hidden among the crop, though from what I saw, if this precaution is taken because of their fatally attractive beauty, it is a hardly necessary one. But to resume. After many hours of such journeyings we at last reached the foot of a steep ascent, at the top of which was our destination, Olting-Thang. Already weary, we started up this hill with a broiling sun full on our backs and eventually reached the camping-ground, quite ready to have a bath, eat the evening meal (hardly to be dignified by the name of dinner when it is over before sunset), and to turn in as soon as it got dark. On the following day (June 2nd) we reached the Indus Valley. Starting along the usual boulder-strewn slope, but now at some considerable height above the river, after about an hour's journeying, we came to a high corner above the place where the Dras River joins the Indus. I looked with some curiosity on this, my first view of the famous valley. The river itself was in no wise like the comparatively clear mountain torrent of the Dras stream, but flowed onwards in a swift, if somewhat sullen, volume of mud-coloured water. At this season the snows are melting rapidly, and a large quantity of sand and mud is swept down from the deserts of Thibet to make the fertile plains of the distant Punjab. If we filled a tumbler with the water and allowed it to stand some little time, we found a deposit of sand quite half an inch deep. The valley itself is of course much wider than that of the Dras, but the tremendous rock "parris," which might be described as the ribs of the mountain ranges on either hand, come down to the stream, usually ending in steep precipices.

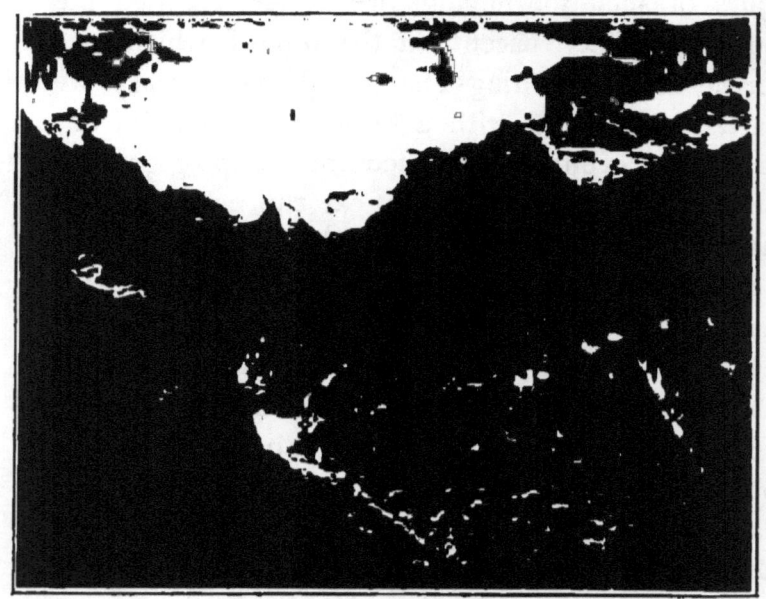

BALTI ROADWAY.

Between these "ribs" are stretches of sand, and wherever a side ravine sends down its stream, the "fan" is cultivated, and a village established. We henceforward lost, to a comparative degree, the oppressive feeling of being shut in by walls of rock, as whenever we were high above the stream our view was bounded by peaks still covered with snow. But the road! One does not expect a twenty foot highway in the Indus Valley, but here the path seems always to be either crossing a slope composed of boulders of every size or deep sand, or by way of variety crawling round the "parris" by means of the galleries already described, which are here more precipitous and rickety than ever; in fact, it was no unusual experience to find that, as one placed a foot on the flagstone which was poised on the precarious wooden scaffolding, it would tip up, affording an excellent view of a sheer drop of some hundreds of feet into the seething torrent below. To add to the comforts of the march, owing to the height of the river, which was now at about its full flood, the road (save the mark!) was in many places submerged or carried away altogether, necessitating a climb of some hundreds of feet over a rocky crest without even an apology for a footpath, a fact which added some miles to the advertised distance of the march. However, though the progress for the next few marches was to be similar in character, this day's work was the worst, and it is always comforting to have the worst behind and not before.

A CORNER ON THE INDUS ROAD.

A SUMMER IN HIGH ASIA.

It was during this march that my retainers saw for the first time my Etna, with which I used to make myself a cup of Bovril (which I found quite invaluable on these occasions, as with an Etna, Bovril, and a couple of biscuits, you are independent of other food for many hours). They could not at all understand why the water boiled, as they could not see the spirit-flame, until I induced one of them to substitute his hand for the saucepan—he understood! Henceforward they always alluded to the Etna as "jadoo" (magic), and I did not undeceive them, as it gives one a sort of prestige to be a magician! This night we rested at Tarkutty, and the following day (June 3rd) our experiences were of a similar character, though one circumstance occurred which made no inconsiderable difference to my feelings. Riding wearily along on my wretched broken-kneed pony through the deep sand under a broiling sun (a pony here is not much good, as he refuses to go up the staircases over the "parris," and you cannot ride him down them), I came round a corner and met two coolies laden with some of the finest ibex heads that it has ever been my good fortune to behold, and greatly superior to any of the many similar loads that we had encountered on the road. The usual question, "Whose were they, and from what nalah did they come?" "They were W. Sahib's, and from the Hushe Nalah. "Was he going to leave it soon?" (this eagerly). "Yes, in about a fortnight; he had got many heads like these." Immediately all thoughts of discomfort vanished; fervent sun, deep sand, rocky parris were all forgotten, and I felt as if I could have done a dozen marches that day towards the Hushe Nalah! However, by the time that we reached Kharmang, or, as it is sometimes called, Khartaksho, we were not sorry to camp. This very picturesque place is of some importance, and is governed by its petty Rajah. We saw the village on the opposite side of the river,

"JHULA" BRIDGE AT KHARTAKSHO.

which is here crossed by a "jhula" bridge, with its fortified palace perched high up on an isolated rock; the Rajah, however, wisely prefers dwelling in a commodious residence situated below in a fertile "bagicha," or garden, to climbing up and down a perpendicular precipice whenever he wants to take a walk. A word about the "jhula," so often described by the traveller in the Himalaya. It consists of a strand of birch or other twigs some six inches in diameter, fastened to piers of stones on either bank of the river, and hanging in a curve more or less slack; on this you walk, while on either side are hand-ropes kept in position by a V shape of sticks placed at intervals; these, in turn, are kept stiff by a cross-piece fastened to them some two feet above the foot-rope, a contrivance which renders the crossing something of an acrobatic feat, as it is necessary to step over these cross-pieces; whilst the excitement is sustained by the fact that you are above (generally very little above, when the middle of the jhula is reached) a roaring torrent, and probably the whole fabric is swinging gaily

JHULA BRIDGE OVER RIVER INDUS.

from side to side in the breeze. The descent on the near side of the curve is the worst part; during the ascent on the further side I found that one usually went much faster! In Pangi once the natives told me that the mountain sheep would cross a short "jhula"—clever sheep! The "jhula" at Kharmang is a long one, and the road down the valley usually crosses it to the right bank, recrossing by another jhula at Tolti, the next march; but on this occasion the natives said that owing to the river being in flood we had better keep to the road on the left bank.

Having heard that the Khitmutgar of a friend of mine, when accompanying his master along this road, had refused, point blank, to cross the jhula, and had eventually to be blind-folded, and, after having been bound hand and foot, was carried over on a coolie's back, I chaffed Sekour Khan (the servants had arrived in camp some time before me), telling him that it was lucky for him that he would not be obliged to cross it, or the same steps might have to be taken in his case. "Yes, sahib," replied this grave Mussulman, "but I have already been across and back to see what it was like!" I said no more. I sent my Perwanas over to the Rajah, who returned his compliments, and said that unfortunately he was too unwell to come and visit me (for which I was not sorry), but he begged my acceptance of the customary "Dali," or present, of dried apricots and currants. Running up from the Indus, behind Kharmang, was an inviting-looking nalah, which, I was told, led by a pass to Kapalu, on the Shyok River, exactly opposite the entrance of the Hushe Nalah. This was said to be full of ibex, but the Rajah allows no one to go there, as he keeps them all for himself (and, indeed, I don't blame him), and kills them by driving, which is the usual way amongst the natives of these parts. The following morning my camp and most of my baggage had just started, and I was breakfasting in the open, when a sudden loud report startled me, and looking up I saw all the retainers running for their lives, and calling out to me to do the same; I did, and then saw some tons of rock bounding

INDUS ROAD, "BETWEEN KHARMANG AND TOLTI."

downhill towards the site of our late camp; the bigger rocks stopped short, but a rain of smaller pebbles went whizzing past which would have made things decidedly lively had we still been there.

In this country one should always be careful to pitch camp where there is no danger of these stone

A SUMMER IN HIGH ASIA.

avalanches, which seem to be of frequent occurrence, more particularly in wet weather. That day the march was very similar to the previous ones. We had one very long and stiff ascent, and when we got to the top found that there was no water for the coolies, who were now pretty well done. The servants and myself had our chagals (leather water-bottles), and fortunately not long afterwards we came to a Dāk hut, a stage for the mail-runners, and here they had some snow stored for drinking purposes, so that the thirsty coolies were able to get some. For a long way our road led over a barren and stony upland, with no vegetation save the sparsely-growing Eurotia; but even this sort of ground was preferable to the eternal "parris." Eventually we made a very steep descent to the village of Tolti, part of which lies in so narrow a ravine that the sun only shines on it for ten days throughout the year. Here there was a pleasant and shady encamping-ground. The Rajah (they have one here also) came to pay me a visit and had tea with me; he, or rather one of his suite, produced his own cup made of green soapstone or jade from which to drink. According to Oriental etiquette he produced a rupee as a token of friendliness, which was only touched and returned (I once knew an officer, lately arrived in India, who, ignorant of this custom, pocketed the proffered rupee, much to the astonishment of the Oriental who had offered this polite token of subservience).

A SUMMER IN HIGH ASIA.

The Rajah of Tolti was very civil, doubtless the effect of "perwana." The village seemed a flourishing one, and there was a large polo-ground, which is to be found in every Balti village where there is sufficient level space. It was much warmer here, and there were mosquitoes.

I had before this discovered a way to defeat the other plagues which had made life a burden, viz., by tying up my sleeping-garb, previously well sprinkled with Keating, at the wrists and ankles. The next morning the Rajah sent me a bunch of roses and a horse to ride as far as the next halting-place, a pleasant change after the native ponies. The road was typical Indus Valley as far as the next camp, Parkutta, but there were fewer galleries. In one place, as I came round a corner, I saw Babu Lal, Sekour Khan, and a coolie climbing on all fours like monkeys along some dangerously steep rocks above the river, and on looking at the road saw that the reason of their doing so was that the track disappeared into the roaring torrent. However, not feeling inclined to climb the "parri" if it could be avoided, and having the horse with me, I tried the depth, and found that the road was only submerged some three feet or so. I waded, and was glad that I had done so, as the horse plunged, lost his footing, and, had I been on his back, I should in all probability have sought the bottom of the Indus and been no more seen. About here the cultivation becomes more frequent again, and besides the wild roses which were in full bloom, I noticed one tree with a very sweet-smelling blossom like a mimosa, off which the natives broke branches, which they stuck in their caps. This was the Sarsinh (*Elæagnus Moorcroftii*, Wallich). At Parkutta the Tehsildar brought me a "Dali" of roses and ripe mulberries, the first that I had tasted; these mulberries, which grow on large and shady trees, are a long narrow fruit, somewhat insipid in themselves, but very refreshing when mashed up with milk and sugar. The next march (June 6th) was to finish our journey down the Indus and take us up the Shyok. This latter is a considerable river which, originating in the main range of the Karakoram Mountains, which are to the north of Ladakh, flows southwards, and then, making a curious bend to the west through the district of Nubra, where it is crossed by the road from Leh to Yarkand, flows through a valley so narrow and precipitous as to be practically pathless even for the Balti mountaineers, which is saying a good deal. Below these gorges it is met by the road from Ladakh, which, coming from the south over the Chorbat Pass, meets it near the village of Paxfain, and continues down its left bank. From this point downwards the Shyok Valley resembles that of the Indus for some distance, till, turning to the south-west near Kapalu, the valley widens, and, with the exception of a few narrow ravines, becomes broader and more fertile, and therefore easier to journey along, than that of the Indus, which it joins about half-way between Parkutta and Gol. I had sent men on the previous day to tell the native boatmen to get the rafts ready for me to cross the Indus at its junction with the Shyok, and Salia and nearly all the baggage coolies started early, as I knew that the crossing would take some time.

Leaving Parkutta the road was rather pleasanter and in better repair than usual, and only in one place did we have to take a short (?) cut over a mountain-top because the track was submerged by the flooded Indus. About midday we arrived opposite the point where the Shyok River, here a broad and peaceful, but, at this time of year, rapid stream, joins the former river. I found that the zāks, or skin rafts, started from this point, and were whirled down by the swollen flood till they reached the opposite bank about half a mile lower; here they landed their cargo, and, starting again, reached the hither side some distance lower still. Here they were taken to pieces, brought back over the sand and shingle on the heads of the boatmen, and then put together again and started on their next voyage. Each of these journeys, therefore, took some time; but when I arrived upon the scene some six crossings had been accomplished under Salia's directions, and I was told that all my belongings would be ferried across in three more, so I sat down and watched and lunched, though as there was a breeze blowing my meal consisted as much of sand as of anything else.

These zāks are a curious and not unexciting means of conveyance, more especially when the river is in full flood, as it was upon this occasion. They are formed of goat-skins with the heads and feet cut off, and sown up with the exception of one leg, which can be quickly opened for purposes of inflation, and bound tightly up again; this process takes place repeatedly, even in mid-stream, as one or another skin loses its buoyancy, and reminded me

CROSSING THE SHYOK RIVER ON ZĀKS (SKIN RAFTS).

of blowing out a football. The skins are placed side by side on their backs, presenting a ludicrously helpless appearance as they lie swollen out with four short legs sticking up in the air, and are bound by the half dozen to a kind of hurdle; the raft is composed of as many of these hurdles as occasion may demand. But more curious than the raft itself is the means of propulsion. Six or four stalwart mariners stand or crouch, an equal number on either side, and in the hands of each one is, not a paddle as would be naturally expected, but a pole without any blade to it. These poles, when in deep water, they ply with incredible swiftness, and so direct the course of the raft, chattering volubly all the time, but evidently knowing their business well; in the meantime the unaccustomed passenger probably holds on tight to the hurdle as the raft rocks from side to side in the rapids, and whirls round and round, while the water washes freely over and up between the skins, soaking everything.

Arrived near the bank, the boatmen leap out, drag the raft to the shore, disembark the cargo, cross the river again, lift it on to *terra firma*, take it to pieces, trudge away to the starting-point, where they inflate any of the skins that may have become leaky, tie the raft together again, launch it, and are ready for the next trip. Truly a primitive means of conveyance, but one admirably suited to the character of the streams and rapids on which probably no other craft, except perhaps the Canadian birch-bark canoe, could live. Where the rivers are suitable, and there is plenty of water, long journeys are undertaken on these rafts, and at such times it is very exhilarating to be whirled along, while the banks present a giddy and misty panorama which seems to fly past before any of the details on either side can be realised. When I arrived on the Shyok side I found all my kiltas and baggage grouped upon the shore guarded by the faithful, but disconsolate, Sekour Khan, who had survived the terrors of the voyage, but was now looking as if he heartily wished that he had never started on an expedition of travel and adventure. No coolies had arrived from Kiris, the neighbouring village, though they had been repeatedly sent for, and Babu Lal had gone off to impress them. Armed with my "perwanas," I set off at once along the somewhat hot and toilsome path that leads to the hamlet, and in due time interviewed the "Thanadar" (head man), and brandishing my letters in his face threatened him with all sorts of penalties for disregarding the orders of the Commissioner Sahib, advising him to procure and send coolies forthwith. He procured them. He now asked me to honour the garden of his house by pitching my camp there, which, after some dignified deliberation, I graciously consented to do. Shortly afterwards some of his retainers came to my tent, and, presenting a bouquet of roses, begged me not to be angry with the "Thanadar." I eventually promised (with some reserve, as my baggage had not yet arrived) to overlook his misdemeanours for this once, but I cautioned him that he had better afford every assistance to any servant of mine who might subsequently pass through the village on his way to Skardo, whither I knew that I should be sending for letters, &c., later on. Kiris is a large and fertile village, and here I observed more flowers and birds than I had seen for a long time, the latter including, besides the ubiquitous magpie, hoopoes, orioles, ravens, chiff-chaffs, &c. The next two days' journeyings call for no comment; the first march to Kuru and the next to Karku presenting the same features of broad sandy valley with occasional precipitous ravines. At the latter place we arrived in the midst of a large amphitheatre, so to speak, of magnificent mountains topped by snows, where there were not only meadows with long grass, but even bogs brilliant with familiar field flowers, such as the purple orchis, a truly pleasant experience after travelling through stony wastes under a broiling sun as we had done ever since leaving Dras.

The next march, a short one, brought us to a camping-ground opposite Kapalu, and here I found a messenger whom I had sent on ahead to W. in the Hushe Nalah, bearing a welcome note which bade me come on with all speed as he had had grand sport with the ibex and was about to leave; but, he added, the snows were melting fast, and for some days he had not seen a good head, which was not encouraging. Near the camp I observed some rough scrub in the bed of the river which looked as if it might repay the trouble of beating it for game. Accordingly I organised a drive, and though the Balti coolie proved the most inefficient beater, screaming the whole time at the top of his voice, and running hither and thither in every direction, I was able to add some hares and a "chikore" (red-legged partridge) to my commissariat. Though this was not quite the season to shoot game, I must plead the fact of having to replenish a somewhat depleted larder with whatever I might obtain. The usual road up the Shyok here crosses to the village, or rather district, of Kapalu, which we could see on the left bank, and which appeared to be a most prosperous place for these parts; but our way became a mere goat-track leading along the right bank. For some distance we ascended a very steep path which brought us out on to the top of some tremendous precipices overhanging the river. Here I made my first acquaintance with a frequent feature of this country, steep slopes of shale standing at an angle that I should be afraid to mention (suffice it to say that it is the steepest slope at which loose shale can stand), the stones of which fell away under our feet as we crossed until they took their final plunge over a precipice of some 1000 feet. Some miles further on, the path led us down to the fields of Machilu, the village at the entrance of the Hushe Nalah, to reach which we had compassed so many weary marches. This nalah, or valley, runs almost due north from that of the Shyok, and is between twenty and thirty miles in length. It leads up to the Mustagh group of the main Karakoram range, with whose peaks, which compose the highest group in the world, viz., "K^2 or Mount Godwin Austen" (28,265 feet), Gusherbrum (26,378 feet), and Masherbrum (25,678 feet), everyone who has read Sir Martin

Conway's magnificent work on the country will be acquainted. The latter mountain, Masherbrum, is at the head of the Hushe Valley, and it is from its magnificent glaciers that the Loongma, or river, of the same name originates, its several streams pouring down the many ravines into which the valley branches at its upper end.

Never shall I forget my first sight of this glorious hill; I had been feasting my eyes on the lofty mountains which form the stupendous aisle of the Hushe Nalah, and which, of a height from 15,000 to 20,000 feet, diminished amongst the clouds in the distant perspective, when suddenly through a rift in the mist, far, far above them shone one glittering peak, seeming to reach almost to the zenith. It produced in one a feeling which can never be forgotten, but which it were better not to try and describe. The range that bounds the valley on the east side is composed of a succession of fantastic crags and precipices that fairly took my breath away as I inquired whether it was there that we were going to pursue ibex, and I must acknowledge to having experienced a feeling of relief when I heard that they were too steep for even a particle of herbage to grow upon them, and that therefore there were no ibex there. These crags appear to be of a dolomite formation, and in places present the appearance of organ-pipes surmounted by sharp pinnacles. On the west side of the valley the hills are less steep and are of the type of granite mountain of which we have seen so many lately, viz., rocky "parris," alternating with steep slopes of loose shale and stone which come down the couloirs from the precipices above and spread out into fans or talus, whose skirts are bordered by the boulders which have fallen from the mountain side. At Machilu I left most of my stores, taking only what I considered would be necessary for a month or so, the time which I expected that I should have to spend in the valley before I got the one or two good ibex heads on which I was intent; besides, I could always send down for anything more that I might need. The River Hushe, though it was, even at this time of year, only about one hundred yards across, flows down a broad stony bed in places quite a mile wide, a fact which shows what tremendous floods must sometimes come sweeping down from these giant peaks. On either side, where a supply of

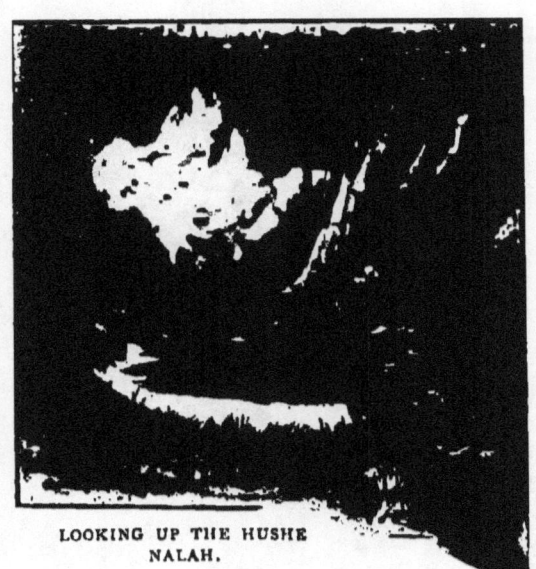

LOOKING UP THE HUSHE NALAH.

water can be obtained by means of the usual irrigation canals, are perched villages, but here they are of a poorer class than those of the main Shyok Valley, growing apparently only sufficient barley and apricots for their own use. A short way up the nalah we passed the opening of the Saltoro Valley which leads eastwards beneath the afore-mentioned organ-pipe peaks, and then, turning northwards, runs up to the glaciers of the main range.

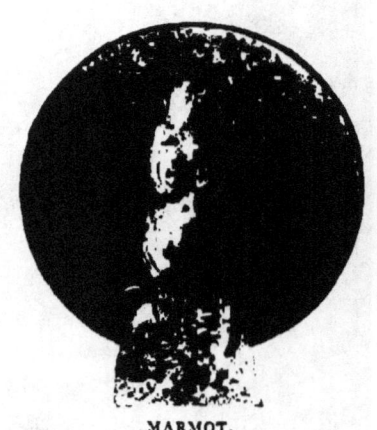

MARMOT.

CHAPTER III.

SHYOK VALLEY FROM MACHILU.

I HAD now, after some three weeks marching, arrived on my shooting-ground, and was longing to let off my rifle, which as yet had not been taken out of its case. My gun had occasionally proved useful, as several times when on the march I had shot some blue-rock pigeons to vary my larder. These latter were in no place very numerous at this season, though I believe that both earlier and later than this they are to be met with almost anywhere in large flocks, more especially just after the barley has been harvested. I had now arrived in the country of the ibex, and eagerly was every hillside scanned in the hopes of seeing them. On the following morning (June 11th) I sent Salia off early with a Balti villager, whom I had engaged as guide, to prospect the country. W. had kindly sent me a note telling me of places where I was likely to see ibex as I marched up the nalah to join him. Starting later myself, I had proceeded some few miles when we met the Balti who had been sent back by Salia, who was exploring the western slopes, with a message to advise me to encamp on the nearest available ground, as he had seen game; also that he was some way off, and that I had

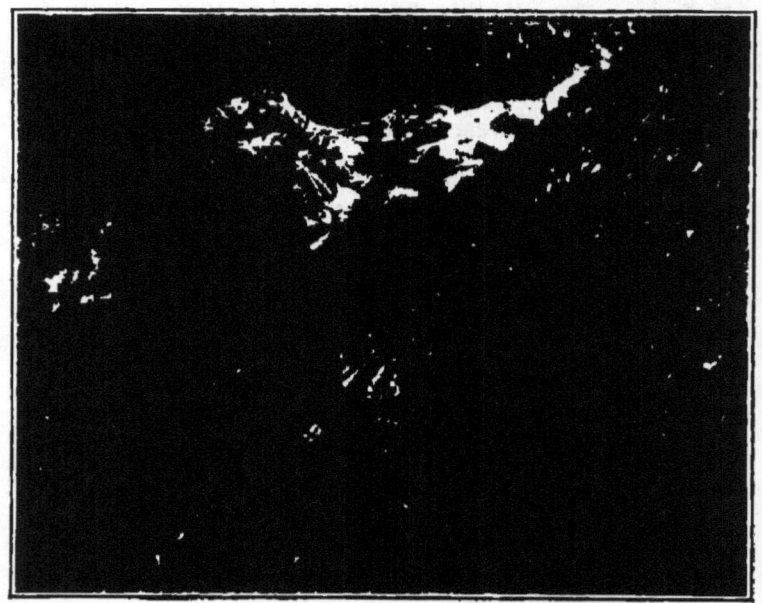

IBEX GROUND.

better wait below and not join him that day. Although burning with impatience, I supposed that he knew best and stopped below, and in the evening he arrived and said that he had seen four female ibex, but no males, and also, far up the mountain, some oorin (*Ovis vignei*). I had not expected to see any oorin, or shāpoo, as they are called in Ladakh, in these parts, and was much excited. The following day it poured with rain and blew a hurricane, making it quite impossible to go out, and I had to content myself with looking up the valley and seeing occasional glimpses of Masherbrum through the clouds; I, however, sent Ullia up the hill, and on his return he said that he had watched a flock of thirty oorin, and amongst them were certainly six very good rams.

Very early the next morning, as soon as it got light enough to see our way, we started. It was my first day's real climbing, and I was not yet accustomed to the rarefied air of these elevations, so that I got considerably "pumped"; while to add to my discomfort my "pulas," or grass shoes, kept on curling up under my feet, owing to the steep angle of the slopes that we ascended, and in spite of the thong which passes between one's big toe and the rest, to facilitate which fastening one wears stockings with the big toe separated, like the thumb of a glove. The hillside that we were climbing was a steep one, and in many places steps had to be cut in the hard sand as if we had been on ice (the mountain staffs used by the Baltis always have a wooden blade somewhat resembling a spud for this purpose). We continued our upward scramble for four hours, and I was not sorry when we reached a ridge, where at last we halted and looked over. There, sure enough, far below us, we could make out two lots of oorin, the first that I had ever seen. Salia now decided that we were not high enough, so off we started again for another stiff two hours' climb up the ridge, at the end of which time we reached the snow. As we lay here, watching and resting, we observed five figures high up on the mountain-side and apparently tending some cows, but examination through the glass revealed the fact that one of them carried a gun and that they were stalking *my* oorin! This was too much! Off set my shikaris to give chase, and off by this time also set the oorin; the shikaris came back again, but the oorin didn't. It was very disappointing after all our toil; however, on thinking it over, I confessed to myself that it was rather hard on the villagers not to be able to chase game on their own hills, though, of course, I did not tell my followers so, but talked long and loud of reporting the case to the Rajah of Kapalu, and of having the whole village put in irons, as it is against the law for any villager to carry a gun or to shoot, if a Sahib is in the valley. However, the oorin had gone, and there was nothing for it but to admire the view, and this I must say made up to some extent for the toil and disappointment of the stalk. Looking up the valley I could see the whole group of the Mustagh peaks, though one or another would become occasionally veiled in cloud. The nearest of them, Masherbrum, rose sheer at the head of the valley, and behind were other peaks which I take to have been Golden Throne, Gusherbrum, and K^2. On the opposite side were the organ-pipe mountains, while some three or four thousand feet almost sheer below us, our camp looked like one white speck; this speck was my tent, the others being too small to be visible. Whilst we were resting here we suddenly espied a flock of eight oorin lying in the middle of the slope below. They were the first that I had been able to observe fairly close and were all females and young rams; they looked for all the world like red sacks with black heads as they lay there quite comfortable on their sides, with their legs stretched out. They soon got up as the sun gained power, and went off to the shelter of some rocks which projected from the ridge where we were ensconced. This being my first day's stalking with him, Salia was anxious to show me how he could bring me up to game, and off we set down the hillside as fast as we could (a somewhat different pace to that by which we had ascended), and finished by a glissade down a sand slope. Peering cautiously over the edge of some rocks, Salia beckoned to me, and, on my looking over, there, not fifty yards below us, lay the unsuspecting oorin, nor did they perceive us until we threw stones at them, when they were off and out of sight in a minute, but oh! how I wished that they had been the big rams, instead of ewes and lambs!

We reached the tents about 3 P.M., having been

out some twelve hours, and Ullia, who had been sent to prospect in another direction, returned having seen a herd of some thirty ibex, but no good head amongst them. The following day was spent in marching up the valley to the village of Kande. Here, after many endeavours to extract information, an old man eventually told us that a small ravine that we saw opening up to the west, and which was apparently closed by a big mountain about a mile from its mouth, turned a corner and became a large valley which had never yet been explored by a white man (this I believe to have been true, as I found, and found on this occasion only, that the Government Survey was not correct), and was full of large ibex. This was, of course, exciting, and Ullia was despatched then and there to investigate. He returned late, having been for some way up the nalah, and said that he had seen three lots of ibex, and that, though he had been accompanying sahibs for many years, never had he seen finer heads. I could not explore this valley now, as I had promised to meet W. on the following day, and besides, it was really on the latter's shooting-ground, as he had not yet made it over to me. I heard that the village cattle were to be driven up this nalah on the next day, and knowing that as soon as they put in an appearance the ibex would leave for higher regions, I sent for the Lumbardar, and promised much "baksheesh" if he would keep his herds below for another week, by which time I hoped that I might

VILLAGE IN THE HUSHE NALAH—DOLOMITE PEAKS.

CALIFORNIA

have at any rate reconnoitred the higher valleys, after having done which I said that I would return. This he promised to do, and, after renewing my injunction on the morrow, I set out, and following the path which led over a stony plateau, and through a rocky ravine where the going was, to say the least of it, rather rough, eventually reached the nest of mud huts that represents the village of Hushe.

On our way we passed the opening of another valley which runs to the eastward, and which was also said to be unexplored. It looked as if it might be well worth trying. Near the village of Hushe I found my friend W., whom I had not seen for many years, and as neither of us had talked to a white man for some weeks, we found plenty to say. He had had fine sport, and had made the most of his opportunities, the result having been a magnificent bag of ibex, the biggest head of which was the splendid pair of 45-inch horns that I had met in the Indus valley, when on its way down to Kashmir. He gave me all the information that could possibly assist me; but his report, that for several days past he had not seen a big head on the feeding grounds, and that the ibex had evidently left for higher regions, was not very encouraging. The following day we spent together, and on the morrow (June 17th), giving me the nalah with the best of wishes for good luck, W. departed southwards on his way to Kashmir, while I set off for the head of the valley, determined that if the ibex had gone high I would go high too, and that it should not be for want of trying if I did not get one or two good heads. A rather amusing incident occurred before we parted. W. and I found that the time by our watches varied, his being about an hour in advance of mine. We each maintained that we were sure that our own time was the right time, he saying that a second watch of his, that had never been known to go wrong, made it exactly the same as the one that he was showing me, whilst I quoted Babu Lal's to back me up. After a somewhat animated discussion, and some thinking over it, with the help of a compass, a stick, and a plumb-line (the latter to keep the stick upright) we rigged up a rough sundial, agreeing that when the shadow of the stick coincided with the N. and S. line, it should be 12 noon. My watch won, being only a few minutes out, but I think that what vexed W. most was the fact of his having retired to rest an hour before he meant to do so, and having got up an hour too early; especially the latter! I subsequently checked my time by this rough method about once a week during my wanderings. The village of Hushe was in itself interesting as a type of the home of the Balti mountaineer who dwells in the more secluded valleys. Shut in on either side by precipitous and forbidding crags and dominated at the head of the valley, some three miles away, by the glaciers and precipices of Masherbrum, the inhabitants pass their existence in a cluster of huts, resembling nothing so much as boxes made of mud. Round the village are the terraced fields, extending from the cliff on the one side to the gorge of the torrent on the other, a stretch of perhaps half a mile of laboriously cultivated ground, producing a crop which mainly consists of "grim," a sort of stunted barley. A certain number of flocks and herds, that is, sheep, cattle, and goats, belong to the villagers, and as the snow melts these are driven up to the higher and better pastures as they become uncovered by the melting snow; and these little black mountain beasts are literally the *bêtes noires* of the hunters of ibex, as these latter of course leave the slopes as soon as the herds with their herdsman and dogs appear. The people themselves are, beyond description, filthy and poverty-stricken, and what their life must be during the long winter months is awful to contemplate. I was told by my servants, however (I did not verify the statement), that these villagers are possessed of an enormous quantity of gold-dust which they obtain from the river; possibly this might prove to be a veritable Pactolus if properly exploited. These villagers told me that they did not care for the "Sahib Log" coming to shoot, as, though, indeed, they got money by their doing so, yet money could not be eaten, and, as they were only able to grow sufficient food for themselves, it came rather rough on them to have to supply the successive retinues of "Sahibs" who came here. I suggested that the money thus obtained might procure food in plenty from the villages in the neighbouring and fertile Shyok Valley, but this fact did not appear to have struck them in their primitive innocence! Amongst the villagers was an old, very old, blind beggar, more like an animated (slightly) bundle of rags than anything else, who used to crawl out when the sun got warm, and squat down near my cooking tent. Regarding him as a sort of guardian spirit of the valley, I propitiated him with small copper change, to bring me good luck, and this act, I am certain, produced the wonderful results to be hereafter mentioned. I took with me from the village two natives, who were to act as guides in the neighbouring ravines, and had been employed in a like capacity by W. who had recommended them: wild-looking fellows enough they were, their hawk-like faces with the straggling elf-locks falling on either side, being quite in keeping with the rocky solitudes amongst which they had been bred. After following the valley for some miles, there are three ravines which all look good to hold ibex; the one straight in front, that leads northwards, being filled with a glacier coming down from Masherbrum. To the west is a long valley very stony and (for Baltistan) fertile, with many birches, cedars, and "bik" trees growing near the torrent; but as this had been shot lately by W., I chose the one leading eastwards. The road follows the left bank of the stream for some three or four miles with cliffs rising almost sheer on either hand, one crag standing out particularly, like an isolated buttress about 1000 feet high, from the Mass of Masherbrum, with sides apparently perpendicular, though there are slopes of grass on the top. "What should we do if we were to see ibex there?" I asked of Salia. "Leave them," was the laconic reply. This was in a way comforting, as I thought that perhaps he considered this sort of thing easy for ibex ground. Some little way farther on we passed through quite a small wood of the pencil cedar (*Juniperus excelsa*), which here grows to a considerable size, that is to say, not high, but with a trunk of some girth. The wild flowers here were lovely. Roses in full bloom of enormous size and every shade of crimson and pink, wild indigo, several sorts of Myosotis, including the forget-me-not (whose English name, literally translated into Hindustani for the benefit of my following, became "Humko-mut-buljao," which scarcely sounds attractive), several Alpine blossoms, such as edelweiss and gentians, and many others whose names I do not know. A little way farther on, this side valley divides into two branches, the one running due north and being filled with a large glacier leading up to Masherbrum and other lofty peaks, while the other runs southeast to another range, the latter being also filled with a glacier and dominated a few miles farther on with some of the most stupendous precipices that it

A SUMMER IN HIGH ASIA.

has ever been my fortune to behold. We camped at the junction of these three valleys where there was some level sandy ground strewn with huge boulders and where many cedar-trees were growing.

All the following day the rain poured down

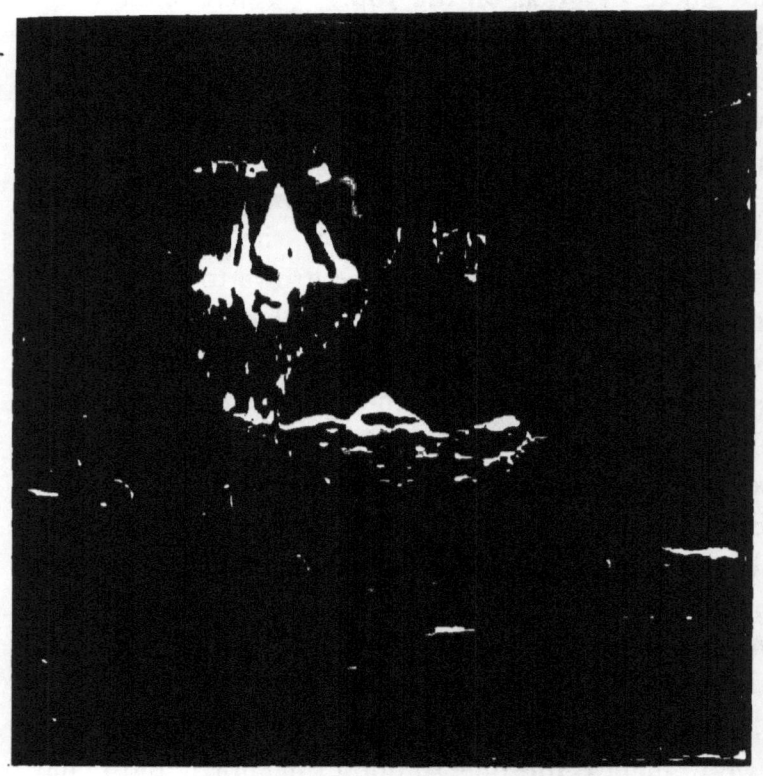

SIDE NALAH OFF THE HUSHE VALLEY.

unceasingly, and continued to do so throughout the night. I was much startled at first on hearing sundry loud explosions, followed by a rumbling sound, which lasted sometimes for several minutes together. From glimpses occasionally obtained through the rain-mists, I found that the cause of these alarming noises was a series of rock avalanches. The overhanging crags split, as I suppose, by the winter's frosts, and then loosened by the heavy rains, came thundering down the gullies and out on to the fans of *débris* which are such a noticeable feature of these rock-strewn valleys. One soon gets accustomed to the noise oneself, but it was some time before I could allay the fears of Sekour Khan, who was fully persuaded that our camp would be overwhelmed; I pointed out to him that we were quite safe, being, as it were, out in the middle of a basin. The noise caused by these rock-avalanches can only be likened to that made by the passing of many heavily-laden luggage trains, varied with the occasional firing of a big gun. At one time on the following day, I must confess to having felt a little nervous myself, as an entire hillside apparently gave way, and the noise was terrific, the rain at the time being so dense that we could not see anything until all of a sudden tons of rock came bounding into view straight towards us; however, they checked their career long before they reached our ground. What with us was rain, a few hundred feet above us was snow, and this we hoped would drive the ibex down. Nor were we disappointed. As it began to clear in the evening, Salia came rushing to my tent to say that a big buck ibex was standing on a rock looking down into the valley. Unaccustomed, or rather out of practice as I was at spotting them, it took me some time to find him, but at last I did so, just as he moved away out of sight. My mind was at once made up, I would go after him. Salia, however, refused to go, saying that the danger from the still falling stones was too great. I have always found it best to follow one's shikari's advice, but on this occasion it was my first chance; I was tired of staying inactive in camp, and I had not yet had a shot, which must be my excuse for having said, "Never mind, I will take a walk up the valley with you, rifle in hand." This we did, accompanied by Ullia and Umdoo, the latter being the tiffin coolie, surnamed "Bhalu" (the Bear). Of course, when we got opposite the foot of the gully above which we had seen the ibex, I insisted on ascending. To make a long story short, we suddenly caught sight of a herd of bucks which had already seen us, and were moving off rapidly along the rocks, some two hundred yards above us. No time to waste, and I emptied both barrels at them as they disappeared. One staggered, but went on; and, firing at them again, I thought that I heard another bullet tell. However, I found myself seized by the arms and dragged down the couloir and round a corner, and not too soon, as a lot of stones came whizzing by us like shots from a gun, having probably been dislodged by the ibex in their flight. I was back in my camp within an hour, having, as events proved, bagged two fine ibex, one with horns of forty-two inches, while the other one was a unicorn of nearly forty-four inches. This latter had only one horn, the skull being almost smooth where the other should have been. Personally I would rather that he had carried the ordinary complement, as his head looks a bit lop-sided, but the shikaris were delighted, declaring that the fact of having shot him portended great good fortune, and that never had so big a unicorn been shot before; and I verily believe that this superstition made them work all the harder subsequently, as they thought that they were in for a "lucky" expedition. The following day (June 20th) I took it easy, sending Salia with the Balti guide up the nalah that ran northwards from my camping-ground, while I followed him about 1 P.M. The natives told me that a Sahib had been up this nalah some eight years ago, but that no one had shot there since then, and as it led up to the higher feeding-grounds, I had hopes of seeing ibex.

Almost as soon as I left camp I got on to the glacier, which comes down in an unbroken stream of ice from the eastern slopes of Masherbrum. To the right, or eastern side as I went up, were high crags, with fairly easy rock-strewn slopes below them; but the precipices on the opposite side of the glacier, a main spur running down from the peak, looked quite unscaleable. Making our way for some distance up the rocky moraine we came upon Salia. He had seen some ibex on the slopes above, but on investigation they proved to be mostly females, with no big bucks amongst them. Not long afterwards, however, on the hillside some little way higher up, we saw a sight to make glad the heart of man, or, at any rate, of shooting man. On a boulder-strewn slope, which comes down to the glacier from the precipices above, was what looked at first like a flock of sheep, but which, on examination, proved to be seventeen buck ibex, most of them with very fine heads. As it was now getting towards sunset we thought it best to leave them undisturbed till the morrow, and I hastily despatched a messenger to Babu Lal to tell him to bring up one of the small tents, food, and blankets. He arrived in about two hours time, and we bivouacked under some overhanging rocks lower down the valley and well out of sight of the ibex. I ate some food and lay down half-dressed, and my troubled slumbers were peopled with ibex of gigantic size tumbling down unspeakable precipices. By 2.30 A.M. I was on my way towards the slope where we had seen the bucks on the previous evening, as I was determined that I would not miss my chance by not being on the ground before the ibex, which were almost certain to return to it as they had not been disturbed. What a scene met our eyes as we set out! The moon, which had not yet set, shed a flood of brilliant light over mighty Masherbrum and its glittering glaciers which towered above us; the crags on our side of the valley were plunged in the deepest shadow, while, in spite of the moonlight, the stars shone out with the strange brilliance that is only to be seen in a rarefied atmosphere such as this was. Not a sound broke the intense stillness save our own footsteps and the trickle of water and occasional fall of some stone into the abysmal crevasses of the glacier on our left; the whole scene produced an impression of stupendous grandeur that seemed almost supernatural. Before starting I had made a hasty meal of hot cocoa and two boiled eggs, or perhaps I should say of one of the latter, as the second, on inspection, proved to be, to say the least of it, "advanced," and this at 2 A.M.! As we were making our way along the edge of the glacier the moon set and the day began to dawn behind the peaks on our right hand. At this time we had to do a rather awkward bit of scrambling over the loose stones of a side glacier that comes down from the east. Jumping from one rock to another in the dark, especially when, as often as not, the one upon which you are for the moment poised, like a performing goat on its ball, shows a decided inclination to topple over, is not the pleasantest mode of progression. Many and frequent were the tumbles, and many would also, doubtless, have been the objurgations, had we not felt that we might now be close upon the ibex; so we suffered in silence, and finally reached the foot of the slope upon which we had seen them the previous evening. After climbing some little way we stopped to take breath, and never shall I forget

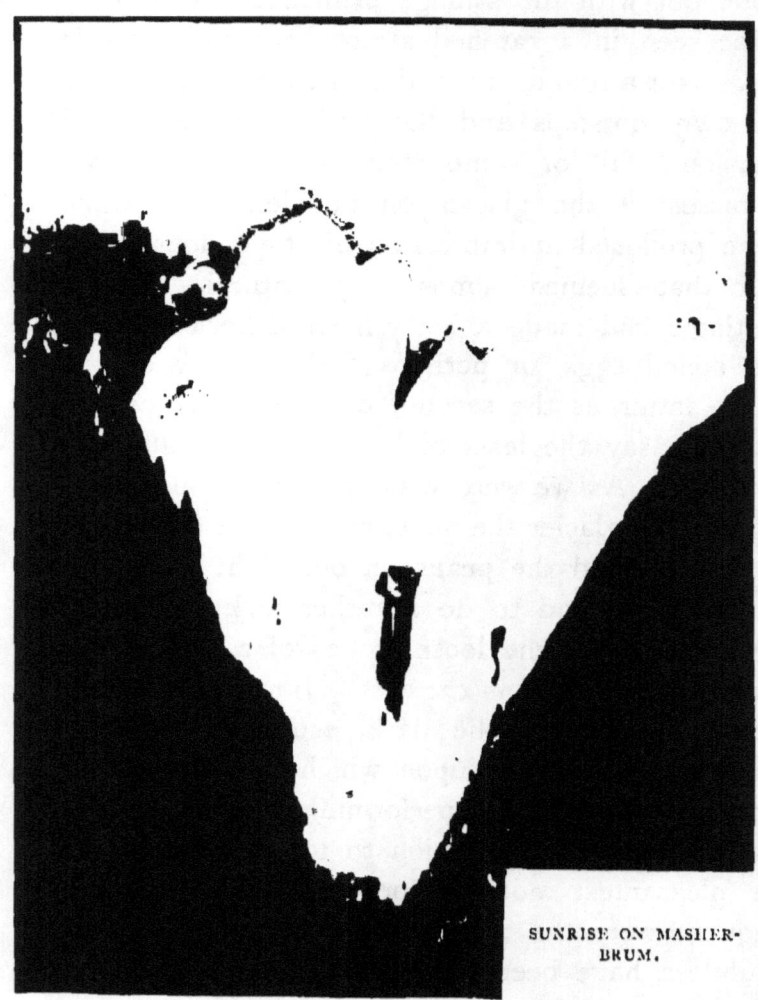

SUNRISE ON MASHERBRUM.

the sight that we gazed upon. If Masherbrum had looked beautiful by moonlight, how magical did it now appear. The whole valley was plunged in the blackest darkness, and the sky was still that of night, but above us rose one mighty peak, as if illuminated by crimson fire, the summit of Masherbrum touched by the rising sun still low behind the eastern range. However, there was not much time to rhapsodise, and we continued our way up the slope. As day broke Salia's experienced eyes distinguished several grey specks amongst the rocks above, which he said were the still sleeping ibex. Soon the females and young bucks awoke and came skipping down the face of the precipice, the latter butting at one another in play and frisking about as they descended to the feeding-ground. We now worked some way beyond, and climbed till we were slightly above them. The wind was at this time blowing down hill, but Salia's knowledge told him that as soon as the sun touched our side of the valley the breeze would change and blow up hill, which would be favourable for a stalk. Accordingly we crouched under a rock and waited, watching for the big bucks to come down. "We" consisted of Salia, the Balti guide, myself, and "Bhalu," the latter carrying food. How long we seemed to sit there, and how cold it was, and how I watched the sunshine creeping across the valley and lighting up first the precipices of the opposite side, then the glacier and its pools, turning these latter to brilliant blue as it passed, and finally climbing our hillside as the sun rose above the peaks behind us. True to Salia's prediction the wind changed, and after some little time the old bucks appeared, coming leisurely down from rock to rock and looking suspiciously around them; there were ten of them, all carrying good heads. They disappeared behind a ridge, and we set off in their direction, crouching low to keep out of sight. We eventually reached some stones, and, taking off our caps, cautiously peeped over. There they were, feeding unconsciously some two hundred yards away at the foot of the perpendicular rocks. Salia whispered to me to come with him, and we wriggled along flat on our faces to a big rock some fifty yards nearer. "The dark one is the biggest, shoot him first," whispered Salia. It was a critical moment as, after a minute's pause to take breath and steady myself, I raised my rifle and fired at the big one—down he came sprawling on the ground—while the second

"THE OLD BUCKS APPEARED."

barrel hit another, who stumbled on to his knees and went off. Hastily reloading, I fired at a third as the herd vanished round the corner, and heard the bullet tell. By this time the females and a few bucks who were with them, alarmed by the noise, came rushing up from below; I fired at a big one, but am sorry to say that by this time I was so excited that I missed him and sent a small buck crashing over the precipice on to the glacier below. All this in shorter time than it takes to write it. In the meantime Salia had rushed forward to "hallal"* the first one before the latter breathed his last, so as to make the meat lawful for good Mohammedans (*i.e.* himself) to eat, when, to our disgust, he sprang to his feet and followed the herd. At this moment a lot of does and small bucks, one of the latter carrying a fair head, rushed past within fifty yards. I fired at this last as he departed and hit him hard. He took to the precipices above. Here he lay down on a ledge, and the Balti, after a perilous climb,

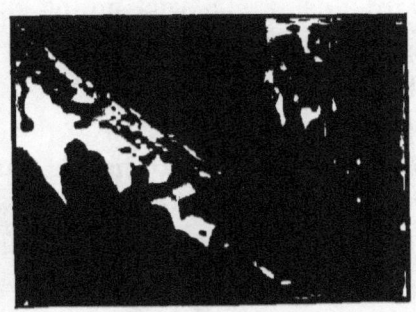

"I RAISED MY RIFLE AND FIRED AT THE BIG ONE."

* Unless the throat of the animal is cut while still living, the good Mussulman will not eat him, though I *have* seen an animal "hallaled" some considerable time after he had breathed his last!

was just about to catch hold of him when he got up and bounded down the sheer rock straight towards us. He was going slow, and "Bhalu" caught him by the hind leg, but was sent sprawling with a kick, and it was some minutes before Salia caught him by the horns, as he floundered in deep snow, and despatched him in the orthodox manner. On following up the others we could see two of them lying on the glacier far below, and the other two had taken to inaccessible places as is their wont when badly wounded : these we had to leave till next day, when they were retrieved. Thus ended a very lucky stalk, and, as Salia said with some pride, "We had at least one hundred pairs of eyes and ears matched against our four, and had fairly defeated them on their own ground."

We did not reach the main camp till 2 P.M., doing the last part of the march under a broiling sun. The delight of the retainers was extravagant, and they caroused far into the night, singing and feasting on ibex flesh. I cannot myself imagine anyone eating ibex unless he was absolutely dying of starvation, for even on approaching an old buck you perceive that he is decidedly "goaty," but to eat him, ugh! However, the natives like the flesh, and I have even seen them greedily devour the meat of a tahr, which is, if anything, more so! On my measuring them, the heads proved to be forty-two and a half, forty, thirty-nine, and twenty-nine inches respectively, the latter being that of the small buck that was shot by misadventure. Having now got more heads than I expected or, in fact, wanted, I determined to leave the ground (though had I stayed, I should, I think, have got a shot at many more good ones), and, after paying a visit to the untrodden nalah that I had passed on my way up, to make my way eastward along the Shyok River and over the Chorbat-La to Ladakh and the haunts of the *Ovis ammon*. Accordingly, having got my ibex, and not being pressed for time, I lingered for two days in this lovely spot, sketching and taking things easy; my dāk (mail) had arrived from Skardo, so that I had no lack of occupation, with letters to write, papers to peruse, &c. It may not be out of place to state here, as showing how anyone journeying in these parts need not be entirely cut off from the outer world, that, by taking in a paper published in India (which has, of course, the latest telegrams), and arranging so as to always have one coolie bringing the mail up from the nearest office while another is on his way to fetch the next lot, one need never be at any time more than one month behind civilisation, though, of course, if one goes very far afield one's news becomes proportionately older. This rest was very pleasant after the continual marching, and, as my tent became unbearably hot during the middle of the day, the handy Babu Lal rigged me up a sort of summer-house, composed of cedar-boughs with a roof made of a waterproof sheet, to keep off the rays of the sun. On the 24th of June I made my way down the valley, with the comfortable feeling that I was already possessed of seven ibex heads, instead of having had to work hard for many weeks for one or two, which was what I had expected. That evening we halted at the village of Hushe, and on the following day arrived at the village of Kande, whence I was to explore the unknown nalah !. On the morning of June 26th I started up this valley, expecting great things. I found on this occasion, the only one during the whole of my trip, that the Government Survey Map was incorrect. The entrance to the valley is most curious. It runs east and west, and looks as if it were a narrow nalah about a mile long, and closed by a big mountain; however, the volume of water pouring down the stream denotes a ravine of some length, and indeed, on reaching the head of the apparent "cul-de-sac," you find that the river takes a bend at right angles, the valley running about north. For some way our path was difficult, as, owing to recent heavy rains, the track had been washed away, and in many places steps had to be cut across landslips which made the going somewhat risky. However, all the coolies and baggage arrived safely if somewhat tardily, and we emerged on to a green plateau where another valley came down from the westward, and where there were traces of former cultivation. Here we pitched camp. It was a lovely spot; the pencil cedars and "bik" trees

A SUMMER IN HIGH ASIA.

(looking rather like a willow) grew in profusion amongst the boulders that had fallen from the precipices above, and the sward was carpeted with wild indigo, various kinds of vetch, many alpine flowers, gentians, edelweiss, potentillas, forget-me-nots, a beautiful sweet-scented columbine (*Aquilegia*), with pale lilac and white blossoms, and a flower unknown to me, which looked rather like a

VIEW IN SIDE NALAH OFF THE HUSHE VALLEY.

small yellow calceolaria. It was on the slopes opposite this camping-ground that Ullia had seen the fine ibex of which he had told me, when I sent him to explore the nalah on my way up the main valley. The Lambadar of the village had, marvellous to relate, kept his word, and had not allowed the cattle to come up and disturb the game. Nothing was, however, visible from the camp that day, but Salia, who had gone up the valley to prospect, returned in the evening and reported having viewed two lots of ibex of fifteen and forty, with some good heads amongst them. Accordingly the following morning I took the small tent and food for two or three days, and started for higher ground. Soon after leaving the camp the valley turns to the north-west, and after a scramble of some miles over loose boulders, we camped in the middle of quite a wood of bik and birch-trees, the most fertile wild spot that I discovered in the whole of my wanderings in Baltistan. From the crags above us on the north side, several magnificent cascades fell into beds of snow; the southern range was precipitous and stony, while the end of the valley was closed by huge glaciers coming down from the snowy range above, a view which had probably never been gazed on by the eye of white man, which made it the more impressive. Whilst we were watching in the evening I was pleased to be the first to descry three bucks with enormous heads appear on the top of a sheer precipice opposite the camp on the

"WE CAMPED IN THE MIDDLE OF QUITE A WOOD."

southern hills, and soon afterwards an excited Balti, who had been sent higher up the valley with Ullia, came running back and reported having seen a herd of twenty-two bucks. As it was just sunset, we determined to leave them for the present, and to pursue them early the following morning. We decided that we would then first turn our attention to the herd, in the hope that the three large ones would reappear the following evening, on the same ground where we had espied them. At 2 A.M. I was called, made a hasty meal, and soon afterwards set off up the stony bed of the river by moonlight. The moraine and rocks at the foot of the glacier were fearful going; however, we toiled onwards for some hours. I noticed a snow bridge, which was quite the most perfect that I have ever seen, and formed a graceful and glittering white arch over the torrent below; it was formed by the junction of two avalanches which had come down opposite slopes, and was therefore different in shape to the ordinary bridge formed by one snow slope undermined by a stream. After a bit we turned up the rocks on our right, and climbed a "chimney," or angle. I began to feel very much done, as we were at a considerable height, but was revived on looking over a ridge by seeing a herd of large ibex feeding

A SNOW BRIDGE.

upwards, and about parallel to us. A short, sharp climb to get above them, and we turned off to our left to intercept them. I peeped over a rock just in time to see a small one disappearing round a corner about twenty yards away; they had got wind of us somehow and were off; disappointing after our very hard work! I ran up as fast as I could, and saw the herd crossing a bed of snow some way above, and with the despairing hope that a shot might turn them towards us, put up my sight for three hundred yards and fired. I saw the snow spurt up quite close to them, and, taking careful aim, fired again and brought one down. This was unexpected luck, though firing at this distance is not to be recommended, more especially at a moving object, as it is much better to leave the game quiet, in the hopes of getting a more certain shot on a subsequent occasion. However, this time I did not much mind whether I got one or not, so it was lucky. The head was a good one, measuring forty-two and a half inches. The return journey was even harder work than the upward climb, as the sun was now high, and clambering over the rough moraines most laborious, and I was not sorry to reach camp about noon, and here I determined to stay in the hopes that the three monsters seen the previous evening would come out to feed again in the same place; but as they never reappeared I fancy that they must have heard our shots in the morning.

The following day I returned to Kande; the

path seemed harder than ever, and on this occasion, and I think on this occasion only, I suffered severely from mountain sickness, experiencing intense pains in my head and limbs, with a most uncomfortable sensation of not knowing when one's foot would reach the ground, such as one experiences in a very rough sea, or (Babu Lal said), like a drunken man. On June 30th we started on our way down to the Shyok Valley. At Machilu, where I retrieved the stores that I had left, I found that the Commissioner's letter to the Tehsildar of Skardo had produced an order to all heads of villages to help me, and a letter to the Rajah of Kapalu, who had sent an official to accompany me. A very droll figure was this same official, dressed in coat and trousers and soldier's ammunition boots; he answered to the name of Karim. The Rajah also sent a message to say that he would be pleased to play polo or go out shooting with me. I was unable to visit him, as my way lay up the other bank of the Shyok; but I sent him a hunting-knife, of which I had brought a store for like occasions; this he appreciated, and asked for any picture-papers that I might have; I suppose that he wanted them to decorate the walls of his palace. I sent him some copies of the *Daily Graphic* and *Black and White*. At Machilu we crossed the Hushe River on "zāks," and had a somewhat merry time of it, as the waves occasionally broke completely over us; the Kashmiris were pale with terror, and I thought that it was a little dangerous, as perhaps it was, as we were afterwards told that "zāks" had never crossed here before; but that the Rajah had said that the boatmen were to go where I wanted, and that I had said that I wanted to cross the stream!—so Oriental! Soon after our arrival at a fertile village where we encamped, one of the whirlwinds that so often come on in the Shyok Valley in the evening burst upon us, and it required a man clinging on to both poles of my tent to keep it up; those of the servants and shikaris were laid low. The main road to the Chorbat Pass and Ladakh follows the left bank of the river, but I thought that I should like to try a new way, and accordingly marched on the following day to a village called "Abadon," situated under a lofty cliff, the inhabitants of which were much surprised to see a white man. However, I might have saved myself the trouble of coming here, as there was no practicable road up this bank any farther, and I had to retrace my steps for some distance and cross the Shyok, here quite a calm stream, on "zāks," joining the main road just above Kapalu.

CHAPTER IV.

WILD COLUMBINE
(BALTISTAN).

I TRAVELLED up the left bank of the Shyok by easy stages, being in no hurry. After leaving Kapalu the valley becomes narrow and turns southeast. The track itself is bad in parts, and in many places is carried round the "parris" by means of galleries similar to those on the Indus road; the villages seem large and well-to-do, but the interest of the sportsman is centred in the various nalahs that run up towards the Karakoram (or, to be more accurate, that spur of it which separates the Shyok Valley from that of Nubra) from the right bank. There is no road or even goat-track to many of these nalahs, most of which, presumably, have never been visited by human being. The rock "parris" in most places are terrific, presenting a sheer wall, thousands of feet high, descending to the river. The entrances to the gorges are narrow and precipitous, but doubtless, like so many mountain ravines, open out and become better going as you get higher up them, while in many cases the volume of water in the streams that come down, shows that these valleys must be of some size. The only way to reach them would be by crossing the river on zāks; but I fancy that they would well repay the adventurous sportsman who should be the first to enter them. As we went up the left bank I scanned these ravines, as far as I could, with my glasses, but only saw ibex on one occasion, a herd of eleven; this was more than I expected to see so low down at this season. The best looking of these nalahs are opposite the villages of Do-oo and Kubaz. The weather was, by this time, extremely hot, and marching up the confined valley very toilsome, especially as recent rains had swollen the side-torrents, and in some places carried away bridges, necessitating long détours and occasional wading. The river itself was so full that the stones being rolled down its bed sounded like continual muffled thunder. The vegetation, as usual, was confined almost entirely to the villages, and a very noticeable feature was a thistle that grew almost everywhere, with a head that resembled a huge spiked ball, probably an *Eryngium*.

The villagers of these parts are not accustomed to seeing many strangers, and, fortunately for themselves, are too far away from the Kashmir-Gilgit road to be impressed for forced labour, and perhaps it was these facts which caused them to be, at least so it struck me, of a far more independent and less depressed demeanour than the Baltis farther south. On the 4th of July I camped at the village of Kustang; one march further on, the main road at Paxfain, leaves the Shyok Valley, which above this point is, I believe, impassable, or almost so, even for natives, and turns southwards, following the course of the Chorbat Loongma, or river, to the Pass of the same name (16,800 feet), by which it crosses into the Indus Valley in Ladakh. I determined to cut off this angle, and on July 5th, sending on my baggage and coolies by the main path, I started straight up the mountain behind the village of Kustang, taking the small tent and provisions for four days. For about three hours we climbed gravelly hillsides and stony precipices, and after that our way lay over slopes of grass; but these were very steep, and at this altitude breathing became difficult. There were many flowers on these slopes, amongst them one resembling a white anemone or hellebore (winter-rose), but with the head pendent. We camped that night in a slight depression on the hillside, where there was a creeping willow for fuel, and a tiny trickle of water. The view of the Karakoram peaks immediately opposite was superb. Near our camp were several colonies of marmots, here the yellow or Ladakhi sort (*Arctomys aureus*), not quite so large as the red Kashmiri ones; there were also several coveys of that fine bird the Ram Chukore, or snow-cock (*Tetraogallus Himalayensis*), whose weird whistle sounded in every direction, whilst now and again they might be seen in small companies, flying along the hillside with wings set and long necks outstretched. Though we saw some female shāpoo and ibex here, there was nothing worth going after. The following day we started early, upwards along the slopes, and eventually reached the highest point, where the only other white man who had ever been here (so I was told) had raised a cairn, and had stuck a pole in it, and this latter he must have brought up from below for the purpose. I could not conceive why anyone should have taken the trouble to do this, until they told me that he was "making maps," *i.e.* surveying, and that it was many years ago, probably an officer of the Government Survey.

Certainly this hilltop is a good point from which to take observations, and when I sat down to look at the prospect, I had no hesitation in saying to myself that I was looking upon a mountain panorama which is probably unequalled anywhere. This mountain-top, some 15,000 feet or more high, commands, from its position, a marvellously extensive prospect, as it stands isolated between the Shyok and Indus valleys. The whole of the Mustagh and Karakoram range, from Nagyr to Thibet, stretch before one in an unbroken line from north-west round to the east, prominent amongst

A SUMMER IN HIGH ASIA.

them being, of course, the Mustagh, or "K" group, whilst from the south-east to the west are the snow-clad peaks of the range that divides the Shyok and Indus valleys.

Immediately below us, as we faced north, we could trace the windings of the Shyok River from Kapalu almost as far as Nubra, and to the east and south, at the bottom of precipices, which fell sheer from the point where we were for some thousands of feet, was the road winding up the Chorbat Valley till it reached the snows of the pass that we were to cross. It was a sight never to be forgotten, this unbroken circle of eternal snow, and by great good luck, at the time when we were there, there was scarcely a cloud on any of the mountain-tops. I sketched in outline some of the more noticeable peaks, and with my compass took their bearing, hoping that subsequently I might be able to identify them, as, of course, the Baltis who were with me were worse than useless, and knew absolutely nothing about them. After gazing at this view (which, *mirabile dictu*, seemed to impress even the natives) for some time, we began the descent to the Chorbat road. For some way our path led down extremely steep shale and boulder-strewn slopes, and here I noticed for the first time a fine purple auricula growing under the rocks. Near some shepherds' huts we met Salia, who had gone on ahead and had seen some ibex, and eventually camped opposite a precipitous mountain-side where we hoped that the latter would come out to feed towards evening. In the meantime, however, wind and dust storms arose, and thunder rolled amongst the peaks, a rare occurrence in these regions. We did not see any ibex until it was getting dark, and then there were no heads big enough to tempt me, so we left them alone. The descent of the mountain on the following morning was an exciting one, as the way led us down sheer rocks and precipices where a slip or false step would have hurled us into oblivion; but after some hours of this sort of work, followed by a scramble down slopes of shingle, we eventually reached the Chorbat stream, only to find that a bridge was washed away, and we had to go some two miles lower down before we could cross. At last, somewhat weary, we reached the place where we had told the remainder of the party to encamp and await our coming, but alas! instead of a comfortable camp, nought was to be seen but the ashes of the previous night's fires, and there was nothing for it but to continue our way, *not* rejoicing!

However, we found the camp pitched some few miles farther up the valley, and the comforts of a big tent, hot tub, table and chair, soon revived one. That night it rained in torrents and blew a hurricane; they told me that two men held on to my tent-poles all night; but I slept through it all! The next morning we started in thick mist and cloud for the Pass. After some miles over rolling

Alps, carpeted with turf and bright with flowers, we camped in a lovely spot. Half a mountain had fallen down and dammed the stream, which here forms a brilliantly clear lake, some half a mile in diameter, and in this lake was reflected the brilliant purple, red, and blue of the surrounding rocks, and dazzling white of the snow which came down almost to its edge. The stream enters this lake at its upper end in a cascade, and round the margin is a

CAMP BELOW CHORBAT-LA (STORMY WEATHER ON THE GLACIER).

belt of short, bright-green turf. I was not sorry that the coolie whom I had sent to Skardo for my letters had not yet turned up, and, as I could not cross the Pass without him, I remained for a day in this lovely spot. Being a golf enthusiast, I had brought a driver with me, and a putter, and so, having made a hole in the short turf, I instituted a putting competition for the camp, I should think the first time that the royal and ancient game had been played at an elevation of upwards of 16,000 feet, though Knight seems to have introduced the pastime into Hunza and Nagyr. The prize was won by Sekour Khan, who holed out in five.

I also had a shooting competition with my little ·300-bore rifle; but, at fifty yards range, the only ones to hit the target were my three shikaris, and even they seemed to be puzzled by the Beach and Lyman sights. They implored me to compete myself, and I did so, not without some inward misgiving, that I might miss the target altogether or take ten to hole out; but fortunately my first shot hit the bull's-eye, and I was in the hole in four strokes, so, trying to look as if I always did it like that, I remarked, "That's the way," and rested on my laurels. On this day Saibra, Salia's son, arrived, whom I had left as shikari with B. He had crossed the Pass, which he reported as having very little fresh snow upon it. He brought woeful tales of flood and disaster in Kashmir, and of bridges washed away. He had brought my stores safely to Khalsi, and said that he was the last man to cross the bridge at Kargil, on the road from Kashmir to Ladakh, before it was washed away. Here, he said, Godfrey and some other Sahibs on their way to Leh were on one side of the Sooroo River, while others were on the Ladakh side on their way down, unable to build a bridge owing to the floods. Godfrey's graphic account of their adventures appears in a subsequent chapter. I was glad that

A SUMMER IN HIGH ASIA.

I had chosen the Chorbat road; but my troubles were yet to come! One Sahib, he said, had lost some ponies, with all his heads and much of his baggage, and I trembled for the safety of my precious ibex horns, now on their way to Kashmir.

He also brought me a note from B. with whom he had been, and who had shot an ibex with a head of forty-six inches in the Tashgaum Nalah (the one where the sportsman from Aden had been so unlucky), which head proved to be the largest shot by anybody that season. The letter was full of the praises of Saibra. While encamped here I shot two marmots, but they were bagged with some difficulty, as the first one was not retrieved until the torrent had been forded, whilst the other one went to ground under some big rocks, and was not recovered until Sultana, one of my Kashmiri coolies, had been pushed down the hole head foremost, and then withdrawn by the heels. I found that for marmots my little ·300-bore rifle was by far the best weapon, as, if wounded by a shot-gun, they almost invariably escape. The wild flowers here were most beautiful, and amongst others I noticed a small viola which I saw nowhere else, and in places the ground was covered with tufts of a lilac and a white primula, whose blossoms grew singly, without a stalk, looking like stars on the green tufts. I had intended to cross the Pass on the following day, but the storms were so frequent that the freshly fallen snow would have rendered this inadvisable, so I had to content myself by moving my camp some three miles farther on, to a spot just below the snow-line. My followers at this height began to feel the effects of the rarefied air, and complained of severe pain, more especially in the head and back; Babu Lal and I found that we had not got complete control over our legs, as before described. There is a theory that would seem well worth discussion by those learned in such matters, and which was propounded to me over and over again by the natives of Baltistan, that the sickness and giddiness which is often experienced at altitudes considerably lower than the high passes where perhaps no inconvenience is felt by the same individual, is caused by some aromatic plant or plants.

Authorities such as Drew, in his " Northern Barrier of India," Chapter XIX., discussing this theory says: "Of course, an easy answer to this hypothesis is that the effect is greatest at those heights whence all these plants, and even all vegetation, are absent." Whilst, on the other hand, General Macintyre, in " Hindu-Koh," says: "Although this idea is generally ridiculed by Europeans, it is so universally entertained throughout the Himalayas by the hill-men as to make one almost think that there must be some foundation for it." Personally, I am inclined to think that perhaps the explanation lies midway between these two opinions, and is, that a person already suffering from "Berg-krankheit" is rendered more susceptible to, and suffers from, the pungent odours of these aromatic plants. One of the favourite remedies suggested for want of wind was the smelling of an onion, and it may have been my imagination, but it certainly did seem to me to make one feel less "blown," and as the natives continually practised it also they presumably believed in its efficacy. Drew mentions that the wild onion is one of the plants that is blamed for bad effects, so perhaps the remedy is a homœopathic one! On this day the coolie arrived with my dāk from Skardo, letters and papers being full of the description of tremendous floods below, and doubling my anxiety as to the fate of my precious ibex-heads.

During the night I was awakened by thunder and lightning, hail and snow, but by 6 A.M. the weather had cleared somewhat, and I determined to attempt the Pass, as there was neither firewood nor food for the coolies for another day. We were soon on the snow, but though the slope was steep for a couple of miles or so, during which we must have risen nearly 1,000 feet, it was not so soft as I had expected. The rarefied atmosphere produced various effects on the different persons. The Balti coolies, laden as they were, did not go more than thirty yards or so without stopping to take breath, and encouraged one another by singing and shouting at the top of their voices (hardly, one would have thought, the best way to recover their wind). Some of the Kashmiris felt pains in the head, some in the back, and some in the neck, whilst, for my own part, I suffered chiefly from my face becoming blistered and almost flayed from the glare and the atmosphere. One of my Kashmiri coolies was really ill near the top of the Pass, but recovered sufficiently to struggle over. I saw Babu Lal take off his own thick stockings and give them to this man, almost the only instance in which I have ever seen one Oriental help another of a different race and creed. The scenery of the Pass was a chaos of rocks and snow, and on the top, which consists of a sharp ridge, I saw two little birds hopping about and apparently quite cheery. For some distance before reaching the summit I had observed a beautiful purple auricula, which grew in the snow-water under sheltering rocks. Unfortunately the heavy clouds and mists hid what must be a magnificent view of mountain ranges, more especially towards the north, but we were lucky in our day, as there was neither sun to soften the snow, nor cold wind or snow-storms, which would have greatly increased the difficulties of the Pass. Arrived at the summit we rested for a short time, and I made my entry into Ladakh with a glissade of some 1,000 feet down a snow-slope, an easy and pleasant mode of progression after our toilsome

CROSSING THE CHORBAT-LA (17,000 FEET) FROM BALTISTAN INTO LADAKH.

ascent on the other side. Leaving the snow we reached a broad and grassy valley, carpeted with primulas and surrounded by mountains of the most extraordinary colouring, purple with streaks of red, crimson, orange, and yellow, with bright green grass, and capped with snow.

Our way led across a mountain stream and down a stony slope. Here we met our first Ladakhis, with their queer good-natured faces and little pigtails. Showing their usual disinclination to allow strangers to enter their country, they said that, as the two bridges at Goma Hanoo had been swept away we had much better return to Baltistan; but I flourished my " perwanas " in their faces, and remarked that I was sure that the Commissioner Sahib would be very angry if I was kept waiting, so that the bridges had better be repaired at once; this had a great effect.

We camped that night above Goma Hanoo, and though the rain descended and the thunder rolled, little did I care now that the Chorbat-La was left behind! That night I slept for the first time in Ladakh. I had to stay in this camp for two days, the bridge lower down having been swept away by the floods. I sent up the valleys in the neighbourhood to see if there were any ibex, but the men reported only does and small bucks. I went up the hills behind the camp, where a small nalah comes down, and saw two doe ibex, which came down almost to the village. They soon observed us, and, jumping the torrent—here a fairly broad stream—climbed up the rocks on the opposite side, continually looking back. The shikaris said that they must have been pursued by a snow-leopard to come down so low at this season, and, sure enough, we found his fresh tracks, but no glimpse of the wily beast did we obtain. Though far from rare, this beautiful animal (*Felis uncia*) is seldom seen, and still more seldom shot by Europeans, owing to his nocturnal habits and extreme wariness. Their tracks are common in places, and their presence often spoils sport in a nalah, not only from their frightening away the game, but also from the fact that where the snow-leopard is there the animals will be much more on the alert than usual. At last a new bridge was completed, having been constructed under Salia's directions with a couple of tree-trunks and my spare rope. The chief difficulty had been to get a good foundation on either side, as the flood was tremendous and the boulders were being rolled down the narrow ravine with a noise like thunder. The path having been washed away we had some very nasty rock-climbing, and in one place had to be let down,

"AT LAST A NEW BRIDGE WAS COMPLETED."

dangling over the torrent. However, we all arrived safely, and encamped a little below Yogma Hanoo. The poor villagers were in a dreadful state, two houses and three men had been washed away, and where there had been fertile fields when Saibra had come up only a week previously there was now nothing to be seen but a wilderness of mud and stones. I promised the Gopa or head man that I would report his case on reaching Leh, in the hopes that some of the taxation of the district might be remitted for this year. Many Ladakhis, who had been waiting to cross the stream for some days, took advantage of our bridge to do so.

Below Yogma Hanoo the valley becomes narrow and rocky, with magnificent precipices, but is rather gloomy and shut-in, and we had some difficulty in climbing the steep rocky " parris," and, in places, in wading the stream, the road having been almost completely demolished by the floods. On the morning of the 15th of July we reached the mouth of the nalah, and came out into the Indus Valley, for which I was not sorry. From this point down to a point opposite Parkutta, where I had struck the road on the opposite bank when on my way to Baltistan, the gorges of the Indus are tremendous and almost impracticable, though they are traversed on rare occasions. Near this spot Babu Lal, to whom I had given a butterfly net, with instructions to catch all that he might see (an occupation that afforded him endless amusement), captured five specimens of *Papilio machaon* (the common swallow-tail) with one swoop of the net. On reaching the Indus Valley, the most noticeable proof of our being in Ladakh, the country of Lamaism, was the frequent occurrence of the long piles of "mani" stones. These stones, so often described by travellers, are usually flat and of varying size; an average one would be perhaps some nine inches in length, and on each one is scratched or carved in varying degrees of elaboration, the sentence, "Om mani padmi om" ("Oh! the life in the beautiful lotus, oh!"), or, as it is sometimes translated, "Oh! the jewel in the beautiful lotus!" the mystic formula of the Buddhist. These stones are built up in walls usually some five feet or so high, and perhaps the same in width, which extend sometimes for as much as a quarter of a mile along the road.

Each good Buddhist is supposed to add his stone to the pile as he passes, and this latter has to be left on the right-hand side as you go along, as, if passed by on the left, the inscriptions would be read backwards, and bring harm rather than good to the Buddhist who had deposited the stone. Accordingly there is always a path on both sides of the piles. These stones you have always with you on the main roads in Ladakh, and they generally denote the propinquity of a village. This day, too, I saw, for the first time, "churtens," the burying-places of Lamaism, queer dome-shaped erections of the form so well known to travellers in these parts, with their pigeon-holes in which the ashes of the departed are placed after having been mixed with clay. These "potted Lamas" are sometimes most elaborate, the mixture being formed into discs covered with symbolical figures and even coloured, but the ordinary being is simply made into a shape somewhat resembling a mince pie, and stowed away in the "churten." The Indus Valley is here very wild; the scenery is composed of rocky crags and precipices, with snowy peaks in the distance, and the river itself was, at the time we were there, like a torrent of yellow mud, which tossed its spray high into the air, even in mid-stream, while miniature breakers rolled upon the shore, wherever it was sufficiently level. Our march for that day ended at Acheenathang, a village perched upon a plateau above the river; here were many "churtens" and a gaudily painted temple; here, also, for the first time, I saw the Ladakhi women, but, as I subsequently found out, not first-class specimens. The typical lady of Ladakh is clad in a striped skirt of red and blue cloth, faded according to her age (as I believe that, with the Ladakhis, both men and women, a garment once donned is never doffed again, unless by chance it doffs itself by falling to pieces). Over her fair (!) shoulders falls a sheepskin; this latter she does occasionally remove when the weather is hot; but the most remarkable thing about her is her head. The hair, woven into innumerable small plaits, is gathered together behind her back and finishes in a sort of tail, not infrequently adorned with tassels or bells, while over the ears it is twisted with black wool or fur, into two large circular excrescences (Moorcroft calls them "oreillons"), and the whole is covered by the "peyrāk," which ornament varies according to the status in life of the wearer, and consists of a strip of dull red cloth, some six inches wide and eighteen long, with rows of rough Chinese turquoises sewn upon it, and occasionally cornelians and other stones, the largest of which is usually pendent over the forehead. When the wearer is rich some of these "peyrāks" are very handsome, and even the poorest coolie woman wears one; in her case, probably bedecked with a few indifferent, greenish-coloured stones. The turquoises are brought down by the donkey-load from China, and are of little intrinsic value, being mostly mottled with dark-brown or black, but they look very effective on the "peyrāks."

The next day our road from "Acheenathang" lay along the same sort of wild valley, and, in some places, where the pathway had been washed away by the recent rains, we had to cut steps across the landslips. The scenery about here is extraordinary. The mountains seem to have gone mad, and if anyone were to paint them faithfully, he would certainly be accused at home of having sought inspiration in the brandy bottle. They are of every shade of red, blue, and purple, and the strata are

A SUMMER IN HIGH ASIA.

twisted and serpentined in every direction. After crossing a plateau at some little height above the stream, we descended to "Skirbichian," a most picturesque village of some importance, with its houses perched on crags, as is their wont in Ladakhi villages, and overlooking the fertile fields below, while, in every direction, and picturesquely perched on prominent points, are to be seen the "churtens." A large stream here comes down from a considerable valley to the northwards, and sad were the tales told us of destruction caused by the recent floods. Salia, who had gone on ahead, had just completed a bridge when we arrived. Changing the coolies who had come with us from Hanoo, we continued our way to "Doomkhar," a large village; here, too, we heard that whole villages had been swept away in the side valleys. The Kardar, who came to pay his respects, told us that three "Sahibs" had occupied the nalah which comes down here, during the present season, and had got three ibex.

During the next march I was able to ride once more, as the road becomes better; for this I was not sorry, as the hot marches had begun to get rather wearisome, and I had been walking for a month. The pony that was brought me was a wretched little beast, but, as we went along, a plump and well-fed grey was seen, looking out of his shed some little way below the road. My people promptly impressed him, and on my insisting on their finding the lawful owner, so that I might ask his leave (a proceeding which they appeared to think unnecessary, if not foolish), we discovered that he belonged to the "Kardar," who said that he didn't mind my taking him. The road was of the same barren description, with the foaming Indus on our right hand, and low sandhills, that looked good for shāpoo, on our left, till we reached the fort of Kbalsi or Khalatze which guards the bridge where the main road from Srinagar to Leh crosses the Indus. This fort is of the type usual in these parts, and has been built down on the rocks near the river, so that it is commanded by the higher ground all round. An amusing story is told of this bridge. The first camping-ground on the Kashmir, or rather Baltistan, side, is at Lamayuru, and early in the year an officer, whom we will call A., was encamped there. It was the season when all the soldier officers, simultaneously let loose from India, race for the good shooting nalahs. A sporting fellow will undergo incredible hardships and perform prodigious marches to be the first to arrive at the nalah on which he has set his heart, and, once his tent is pitched, by an unwritten law, which is always rigorously respected, no one else may fire a shot in that valley. Well, A. was at Lamayuru, when unto him came another officer, B., who was also racing along the road. They dined together, and B. confided to A. his intention of taking the Khalsi Nalah, where there are ibex and shāpoo, and asked A. what he was intending to do. "Oh," said

A SUMMER IN HIGH ASIA.

A., "I shall stop here for a day or two and try for shāpoo." However, in the dead of night A.'s shikari came to him and induced him to get up and proceed at once to seize the Khalsi Nalah. He had not gone long when B.'s shikari, who had got wind of their departure, came and dragged B. out of bed, and putting him, as he was, on a pony, started off in hot pursuit. On the road there happens to be a ridge over which a short cut may be taken, but A., all unconscious that he was being raced, went quietly along the main pathway; meanwhile B., going over the ridge, got a good start, crossed the bridge at the Khalsi fort, and persuaded the native soldiers who were on guard to shut the gates of the bridge for a couple of hours, so that A. and his shikari were kept storming, but impotent; and when at length they got through and rushed on to the nalah, they found B., whom they thought to have left behind, sound asleep at Lamayuru, comfortably installed. Of course this is only a story, and must be taken for what it is worth; one hears many such; how sportsmen, racing for some nalah, have lain down to sleep across the road, so as to make sure of being awakened should anyone pass, and been stepped over by their rivals as they slept; or of men being called up in the middle of the night because others were coming, and pursuing their way over deep snow in night-gear and slippers, and such-like tales, which are generally true. Officers who want to shoot are many, leave is short, and good nalahs are few, which accounts for the racing; and it shows what an Englishman will go through to obtain good sport, more power to him! It is, indeed, a healthy sign when our young officers prefer the hardships and victories, or I might even say defeats, of a sporting trip in the Himalaya to any other form of amusement; and as a means of promoting the soldier-like qualities of coolness, self-reliance, and pluck, an expedition amongst the mountains of the Northern Barrier of our Indian Empire cannot be overrated; in fact, the officer who has pursued the wild game of the Himalaya must feel himself more at home when engaged in one of the frequent expeditions against turbulent tribes, which is so often the lot of our soldiers in India, than if he had spent his leave in the plains, or enjoying the more Capuan life of hill-stations.

Perhaps he may find himself stalking human game over the very ground where he has stalked ibex, plus the excitement supplied by the fact that human game occasionally return his shot, which ibex never do! But to return to our journey. At Khalsi there is a clean and comfortable bungalow, built on the rising ground above the village by the Commissioner. This is kept religiously closed, but the "Perwana" proved a veritable "open sesame," and I found myself sleeping that night under a roof, for the first time since I left the Murree road some three months before. I was not sorry that this was so that night, as the rain descended in torrents. The following day I rested here, and looked over the stores brought by Saibra from Srinagar, which he had left in charge of the Tehsildar. Our next march was a long one, being in reality a march and a half, twenty-five miles. At the village of Snurla I changed my coolies, this being the proper "Parao," or march. Continuing for some distance, I met a gorgeously apparelled Ladakhi with his suite. We exchanged greetings, and he told me that a short way further on the road had been washed away, and a short cut had to be taken over the mountains by a path that was quite impossible for beasts of burden; this was pleasant, as I had five yāks, or rather zhos, and a pony, amongst my transport! This Ladakhi proved to be Munshi Palgez, a charming old man and a great shikari, who holds a Government appointment of some importance in Ladakh, and to whom Godfrey had kindly given me a letter. On reading this, he gave me a note to his son at Leh, as he himself was on his way down to meet the Joint Commissioner who was still detained at Kargil, building a bridge over the Sooroo River.

On leaving the road to take the short cut we had some climbing, and then a very steep descent, and equally steep ascent to cross a ravine. The baggage animals managed somehow—I believe that they must have walked up the torrent breast-high in the water. It was certainly a climb, but a Balti would have made light of it. Ladakhis are not so accustomed to bad ground, as their hills are of a different type to the granite crags of Baltistan. The road eventually took us over a high plateau, whence we had a fine view of the promised land Ladakh, a sea of rolling mountains and snowy peaks, ahead of us; and we eventually descended to Saspul, a village of some importance. Encamped here I met P. and C., who had wintered in Yarkand, and were bringing down several fine heads of *Ovis Polii* and other Central Asian game. They had tried to cross the Mustagh Pass from the north, but had been deserted by their coolies, and after severe hardships had reached Leh. We spent a pleasant evening together—they kindly gave me dinner, and I was able to supply them with some newspapers, &c. Amongst other curiosities they were bringing down was a four-horned sheep, one of the fat-tailed sort, from the Pamirs; in addition to its ordinary ram's horns, it had two horns rather like those of an ibex, but straight and some twenty inches in length; it was quite tame and

ON THE ROAD TO LEH. VILLAGE OF SASPUL.

would eat from the hand. The next day we passed through Bazgo, another of the picturesque villages perched on crags which are so common in Ladakh, and here we saw a prayer-wheel turned by water, a convenient way of having one's prayers said for one, as, according to the Lama religion, the greater the number of times that the mystic "Om mani padmi om" is repeated, the more stages you pass through on your way to the attainment of the seventh heaven, "Nirvana." I was unable to ascertain whether this prayer-wheel said prayers for the whole village at once, or was to be hired by the hour.

RUINED BUDDHIST VILLAGE OF BAZGO.

That night we encamped at Snemo, and the following day we started up a path leading at first through many gullies and ravines in the low sand-hills. Here in one place I observed innumerable small heaps of stones piled up in every direction in a narrow defile. On inquiry I was told that these were placed here in order to be handy for the good spirits to throw when attacked by the demons who would some day come down this ravine. I should like to be there to see the battle when it comes off! Still following the course of the Indus we reached a grassy flat below the Gonpa, or Monastery, of Spitak, and here we left the valley and turned northwards along a straight road crossing an extensive, stony plain, at the head of which we could see the trees and buildings of our destination—Leh. Though apparently so close, yet it is in reality some five miles away, and I was not sorry when I found myself at last riding under the archway into the main bazaar of the capital of Ladakh.

"MANI" STONE.

CHAPTER V.

THE town of Leh, or Ladakh, as the natives call it, naming the chief town rather than the district, has been so often dilated upon by other pens, that anything more than a description of it as it struck the writer would be superfluous. From its position, at a point where three great roads meet, it is bound to be a place of some importance, at any rate, during the season that these roads are open and the caravans arriving. Roughly speaking, from the north comes the road from Yarkand and Central Asia over the Karakoram Pass; from the east that from China and Thibet; and from the south those from India. I say those, as there are two roads which are both much used, the more easterly one that from Simla, which, crossing the main range of the Himalaya by Spiti and Lahoul, arrives by way of Rupshu; and the other, the well-known one, from Kashmir. In the bazaar of Leh, therefore, during the summer, you will find individuals of many nationalities who have arrived, after months of travelling over lofty passes and stony wastes, to exchange or sell their goods in this common mart. But of the trade that passes through Leh we will speak later. At this time but comparatively few merchants had arrived, and I did not see the picturesque bustle of this centre of commerce until my return journey, when the town was full of life and local colour. The town is dominated by a palace (the residence of the Gyalpo, or ruling race in times gone by), and the inevitable Gonpa, Lamaserai, or monastery, as we should translate it. The palace is a huge barrack-like erection, standing on a commanding spur, and presents that curious form of building, so common in Ladakh, which slopes inward from the foundations, and reminds one somewhat in shape of the "pylon" of an Egyptian Temple.

The Gonpa is apparently very similar to other "Gonpas" in this grotesque land, being painted red and white, and ornamented with many yāk's tails on poles, and rags on strings, floating in the breeze. The main bazaar is a long and fairly broad street, with open shops on either side, where the merchants of many nationalities ply their trade, and is planted with rows of poplars, each one of which is fenced round with a curious open-work brick erection. The Serai, where the Yarkandi caravans are encamped with their herds of ponies and yāks, is well worth a visit, as also is the Wazir Wazarat's house, which stands in a well-planted "bagicha," or garden. Behind and beyond the main bazaar are the narrow and tortuous lanes of the town, while farther west we come to the dwellings of the Europeans, the houses of the Moravian Mission (whose members, Mr. and Mrs. Weber and Mr. Shawe, are untiring in their kindness, and in doing everything they can to make things pleasant for the European traveller), the Joint-Commissioner's house, which stands in a grove of well-grown trees, and where there are both grass and flowers in the "compound," and the "Dāk Bungalow" next door, which can also boast of a fine row of poplars, and contains three sets of rooms for travellers. The Joint-Commissioner had very kindly given me leave to make use of his vegetable garden, should I be in Leh during his absence, and, as he was unfortunately still detained in making a bridge near Kargil, I took advantage of his kindness.

Never before had cabbages and salad tasted so good; to appreciate green vegetables thoroughly one must go without them for a couple of months or so. For my part, I had been living on potatoes and compressed vegetables ever since I had left Kashmir—the latter a sort of stuff that is very good in its way (you cook a square inch and it enlarges itself into a plateful of chopped-up carrots, &c), but is not quite the real thing; besides, after eating it daily for some weeks, you get rather tired of it. I had fed on the wild rhubarb of Baltistan, which was good but insipid, and on one occasion had even tried grass, not on all fours like Nebuchadnezzar or an Ovis Ammon, but cooked like spinach; I didn't care for it. The day after arriving at Leh, I called on the Wazir and presented Captain Godfrey's letters. He was very civil, offered me a cigarette in a sherry-glass, reminding one of a cheap restaurant, and really did all that he could to help me. He gave me "perwanas" to be read to all head-men of villages, said that he had heard from Samad Shah, my banker in Kashmir, and would be happy to supply me with unlimited rupees, gave all necessary orders that transport should be supplied to me, as well as the store of food that we had to take with us for the retinue (as we were about to plunge into wilds where supplies were scarce), and last, but not least, gave orders for a local shikari, who was said to be well acquainted with all the best shooting-grounds, to accompany me.

This man was an Argoon, that is, the son of a Kashmiri father and a Ladakhi mother, and, though he did not know much about the actual hunting of animals—indeed, Salia would not let him take charge of a stalk—he proved quite invaluable in the way of talking to the inhabitants and interpreting for us, as of course he knew both Kashmiri and Ladakhi, and also made all the necessary arrangements with them for food, &c. He answered to the name of Ramzahn. The remainder of the one day that I stayed at Leh was spent in selecting the stores that I should require for two months or so, and sending the rest of my baggage to the Wazir, who

THE CENTRAL ASIAN ROAD LEADING INTO LEH.

kindly undertook to look after it till my return, and to put it with the State treasure under the charge of a guard (this was a hardly necessary precaution, as it mainly consisted of old clothes, books that I had read, and other such like valuable articles). During the evening the Wazir returned my visit with a ceremony that is truly regal, and still obtains in the East, and we sat discussing the weather and other interesting topics for the orthodox period, after which he mounted his piebald pony (his house was quite two hundred yards away), and rode off amidst the salaams of the natives. I did not start until rather late on the following morning (July 23rd), as there was still a good deal to be done, and the first march is a short one. By the Wazir's orders I had been supplied with an excellent pony, and it did not take long to reach Golab-Bagh, our camping-ground (twelve miles).

Our way led at first along the eastern edge of the Leh plateau, down to the Indus, which we crossed to the left bank. Here the valley of the river is very different to what it is lower down; in fact, we seemed to have entered a new world. Instead of narrow gorges and frowning precipices we were now traversing a broad valley, the mountain boundaries of which are many miles apart. The stone "fans" that run down from these latter descend at a very gradual slope to the river, which is here half a mile across in places, and these slopes are well cultivated and occupied by many thriving villages. Nearer the river are big grassy stretches, on which were feeding innumerable ponies and donkeys.

For some miles our road lay through the fields belonging to the village of Chushot, which were at this time green with barley and bright with flowers, whilst on the opposite side of the river we could see the Gonpa of Tikzay, perched as usual on a high rock, and many villages, while on both sides were stony mountains rising to the snows above. Ahead of us, and far away was the range that separates Ladakh from Chinese Thibet, crossed by the (to Europeans) mysterious and untrodden road to Lhassa. Why this first camping place should be called "Golab Bagh" (garden of roses) I cannot imagine, as anything less like a rose-garden I never saw; it consists merely of a swamp in which grow a quantity of willow-trees, and so wet was it that we had some difficulty in finding a dry spot on which to pitch my tent.

On the following day our road took us to Machalang, pronounced "Marchalong," evidently an invitation to proceed; and the way led over sandy plains with considerable cultivation in places. Particularly did I notice the entrance of a nalah running southwards, which, from the length of the piles of "Mani" stones which bordered the path approaching it, evidently was the road to some large village. I noticed this, but not having a map of these parts, I did not then know that the sacred village of Himis, with its wonderful monastery, was within a couple of miles of me; as it is situated in a side ravine so narrow and rocky that from the main road you see no vestige of it. I had been told when in Srinagar that I ought to make a point of seeing what I thought they called the "Hemisphere." I had not at that time read Knight's book, and knew nothing of the Himis

LOOKING UP THE INDUS VALLEY FROM MACHALANG.

Fair; however, I could not have combined ibex-shooting in Baltistan and this wonderful Buddhist, or, to speak more correctly, Lamaist, ceremonial, and, perhaps it was my bad taste, preferred the former. On my way back I visited this Gonpa, which is well worth seeing, even when the ceremony is not going on. From Machalang there is a nalah, which is famous for its burhel-shooting, by which you can make a short cut over a Pass into the Miru Valley; but as at this time I had not heard of the burhel, and was told that the road was deep in snow, I did not attempt it, but continued my way along the main road to Upshi, at which point we were to leave the Indus Valley. Here, for the first time, I saw those heaps of horns, so common in Ladakh, and which I was so often to scan anxiously in later days, to get a clue as to which game was to be found in the vicinity.

These piles usually consist of a cairn of stones with a pole stuck in the middle of it, from which flutter age-worn and tattered rags of linen or cloth; round the base of this pole are heaped the horns of the domestic yāk and goat, as well as those of the wild animals found in the neighbourhood. These latter, as a rule, are not from the heads of beasts that have been shot by the villagers, for your Ladakhi is no sportsman, but have been picked up in the ravines, or by the edge of some stream which has washed them down from the higher grounds, and have probably belonged to some animal that has died from natural causes, been swept down by an avalanche, or devoured by wolves, wild dogs, or snow-leopards. Many of these horns are coloured red, a fact which, though it may add to their virtues in the sight of a Lama, rather detracts from their appearance as a horn!

The natives told me that all the animals whose horns are thus collected and placed upon the sacred piles, will in time be born again in the Buddhist heaven.

Amongst the burhel horns that I measured from the pile at Upshi, were specimens of twenty-two and twenty-five inches in length, the latter pair having a girth of twelve inches. At the village of Upshi the road from Leh to Simla turns off southwards, leaving the Indus Valley, and ascends through the narrow ravine of Miru, till it comes out on the tableland of Gya. It was in a nalah that runs into the hills from that latter place, and which is named after the village, that I had determined to commence my pursuit of Ovis Ammon and Burhel. Munshi Palgez had recommended this valley to me, though he said that big Ammon heads were here few and far between, and, as I subsequently discovered, the ground had already been shot by three "Sahibs" during the present season; however, it was on my way, and was a good place from which to begin. The natives of Upshi had warned me that the road was very bad, having been swept away by the recent floods; however, I found that the only real difficulty was to be encountered at a place where a space of some twenty yards of the pathway had disappeared, and we were compelled to scramble along some rather bad rocks above the stream. We now began the ascent of the ravine, along the left bank of the torrent, which is here shut in by precipices on either hand. When I attempt to describe this march my pen fails me; suffice it to say that these few miles from Upshi to Gya, of the many hundreds that I have travelled in the Himalaya, stand out alone in my memory as the most remarkable, for the exaggerated quaintness of their scenery. The road seems even to have struck an old traveller like Moorcroft, who describes it with more than usual detail in the account of his travels in these regions, when he was the first European who had been here, now some seventy years ago.

I cannot hope to adequately describe the scenery of the upper part of this valley, or to even give a faint idea of what it is like, but transcribe what I wrote at the time in my diary:—

"The mountains had been for a long time wonderful, but here, after passing through the village of Miru, I doubt if they could be equalled anywhere in the fantastic scene that they present. It is Nature gone mad, delirious. The hills and precipices closing in on the gorge are not of a great height, but the strata of sandstone and conglomerate stand out like huge ribs, some fifty feet or more from the slope and sometimes not more than a dozen yards apart, looking as if some giant hand had built huge, rugged walls, from the summit of the mountains to their base. The intervals between these walls are composed of earth or stones, each one being of some different prevailing colour, purple, green, blue, yellow, white, and crimson. I was particularly taken with a turquoise-blue stripe between two venetian red ones."

I can only add that some months later, after having seen much of the wondrous colouring of the Ladakh mountains and the highlands of Rupshu,

THE TOWN OF LEH.

CALIFORNIA

this fantastic gorge had, to my mind, lost nothing of its singularity; in fact, I think that it then impressed me almost more than on the first occasion that I saw it. After some miles of travelling along this road, which, as you ascend, becomes so narrow in places, that you could with ease throw a stone across it, we eventually turned sharp to the east, and emerged upon the plateau of Gya, which presented to my eyes exactly the scene that I had always imagined the true Ladakh to be like.

We had now left the rugged side nalahs of the Indus Valley, and had come out on to a rolling plateau of stones and gravel, that stretched away in gentle undulations to the snow-fields that surround it to the west and south, and over which the road runs by the Tagalang Pass (17,500 feet) towards Lahoul, and eventually to Simla. The village of Gya is about 13,500 feet above the sea-level, and it is a considerable place, with many Churtens and "Mani" piles. I suppose that the fact that the latter are here more extensive than is the case in most places, arises from the devout feelings of thankful Lamas who have safely crossed the uninhabited and inhospitable regions beyond, for Gya is the last village of permanent dwellings to be met with on this road, and beyond it the traveller sees nothing but the black tents of the nomad Tartar, the only inhabitant of the higher regions. At Gya there are three trees, and these I bid an affectionate farewell, knowing that it would be many a long day before I looked upon another.

There are fields here of the usual terraced order, and short green turf grows wherever there is water, but the only crop that I could discover was "grim" (Siberian barley), which had not yet ripened when I passed the hamlet on my homeward journey in September, when the winter's snows were already beginning to whiten the slopes of the Tagalang. I had hoped to have encamped this night in the Gya Nalah, which turns off to the east some three miles above the village; but, though I had sent Saibra on very early to get things ready, I was disappointed in this, for all the yāks were away feeding on the mountains. The head-man, doubtless impressed by the "perwanas," had displayed more than usual zeal, and had sent off mounted men to bring in these yāks; but, as they could not arrive before evening, there was no hope of starting till the following day. I got hold of a villager who had accompanied the former occupant of the nalah, and he promised to show me both Ovis Ammon and Burhel, which was welcome news.

CHAPTER VI.

The next morning, after marching some three or four miles up the Simla road, I turned off eastwards, and, fording a considerable stream, took possession of the Gya Nalah. Some two or three miles up, this valley divides into two branches, which run almost parallel to one another, and are known by the names of Kayma and Tubbuh. I proceeded up the former branch, which is a typical Ladakhi valley. On either side are hills of many-coloured gravel and shale that rise to a height of some two or three thousand feet above the stream; they are generally rounded in outline, but are occasionally broken by steep, rocky ground and precipices. These rise gradually to the snowy ranges behind them, the snow-line at the time that I was in Gya being at some 18,000 feet (the perpetual snow-line here is about 20,000). In the middle of this valley, which is here about half a mile across, flows a fair-sized stream, the water of which, as is usual in mountain torrents, in the early morning, and while the snows above are still frozen, was clear and good, but towards evening increased greatly in volume and became very thick. At the head of the valley is a range of snow-covered hills.

CAMP IN THE GYA NALAH.

On either side of the stream for some little distance, is found green turf and abundance of wild flowers, while occasionally its waters flow through quite a boggy bottom with tussocks of grass and short reeds, the sort of place where one would make sure of meeting a snipe in Europe, though here I saw none. The yāks luxuriated in the green grass, and there was abundance of fuel in the shape of a low-growing shrub, looking rather like gorse, and called by the natives " Jupsang," or " Dhepsang," and the eternal " Boortse" (*Eurotia*). The northern branch of the Gya Nalah, Tubbuh, presents rather different characteristics ; the water of the stream in

this ravine was of a brilliant crimson, which I found to be the prevailing colour of the mountain at its head, and which was noticed by Moorcroft. The valley itself is much more confined than Kayma, the hills on either side rising steeply from the stream, those on the north being of some considerable height. In many places there are the same little grassy patches as in Kayma; but here they are much smaller and less frequent than in the broader branch. In both these ravines there are lots of animal life. Amongst the birds, I noticed large flocks of snow-pigeons, with their lovely white and grey plumage, ram chukore, ravens, choughs, gelinots, or snow-larks, and many small birds, of whose names I am sorry to say that I am ignorant, besides many vultures, lammergeiers, and hawks of various species. Marmots abounded, of the yellow Ladakhi sort, and one emerged from his burrow close to my tent, and not five yards from where I was lying on my bed, reading. Quantities of mountain hares were to be found on every hillside, and though I found it hard to get near these animals with a shot-gun, they afforded excellent practice for my ·300-bore rifle, and were a very welcome addition to the larder. They are smaller than our English hare, and are ashen-grey on the hindquarters. They are to be found almost everywhere in Rupshu, sometimes in considerable numbers, and, when disturbed, invariably make uphill; I have come across them at an altitude of

16,000 feet, and even higher. Amongst the flowers that I noticed here were auriculas and primulas, myosotis of various sorts, ranunculus, and a plant somewhat resembling a red-rattle (*Pedicularis sylvatica*), of which latter species there was another sort, bright yellow in colour with crimson spots, and a very long "neck." This latter plant was to be found on boggy ground near the stream, whilst on the gravel slopes above were the usual aromatic herbs, southern-wood, eurotia, and wild lavender. There were several sorts of butterflies, which Babu Lal pursued with untiring energy, though running after a strong flying insect at an elevation of 14,000 feet must have been a trifle exhausting. But, what was of a great deal more importance in my eyes, there were both Burhel and Ovis Ammon in the nalah. To take the latter animal first, as, indeed, would seem his right, being, as he is, king of Thibetan game.

Ever since I had fired my first shot in the Himalaya and become a victim to the fascination of what I venture to consider as fine a sport as human being can desire, I had dreamt of getting a good Ovis Ammon head; not, indeed, that I ever expected to do so, as such a stroke of luck seemed beyond the expectations of a humble shooter like myself, but my imagination was fired by quotations like the following from books written by the most experienced sportsmen that ever fired a rifle in the Himalaya. Kinloch, in his magnificent work,

A SUMMER IN HIGH ASIA.

"Large Game Shooting in Thibet and Northern India," says: "The horns of this sheep are enormously massive in proportion to its size, and an old ram's head is *the* trophy most anxiously coveted by the Himalayan hunter, and very often longed for in vain. . . . I have hunted most kinds of large game in India and Thibet, and, after a lengthened experience, I can unhesitatingly affirm that there is no animal so difficult to stalk as a male nyan." To quote the words of "Mountaineer" in the "Summer Ramble in the Hamalayas": ". . . When the successful hunter at length runs up to a fallen beast, lifts up his enormous head and surveys his ponderous horns, he may rest assured that he has gained the highest step in the art of deer-stalking."

Again, Major-General Macintyre, in that most charming book of Shikar, "Hindu-Koh," says: "In fact, the man who fairly stalks and kills his big ram Ovis Ammon may consider that he has gained the 'Blue Ribbon,' so to speak, of Himalayan sport." Whilst Colonel Ward, in his "Sportsman's Guide to Kashmir and Ladak," a handbook which is as indispensable to anyone who shoots in the Himalaya as is his rifle itself, says: "Ovis Ammon are more plentiful than is generally supposed to be the case, but large horns are rarely obtained." Small wonder then that I was excited on hearing that there were Ovis Ammon in the Gya Nalah.

A SUMMER IN HIGH ASIA.

The name "Ovis Ammon," by which this fine beast is most usually known, is a misnomer, the genuine Ammon being, I believe, an inhabitant of Eastern Siberia, while the proper scientific title should be *Ovis Hodgsoni*. But the native name, and the one by which he is known to all sportsmen who have shot in Thibet, is "nẏan," so as nẏan I shall allude to him henceforward. I may here state that the usual Latin name seems to be an insuperable difficulty in pronunciation to the Kashmiri shikari, and after I had spent hours in trying to teach Salia how to say it, the nearest approach that he could manage sounded something like "Oblesimmon," pronounced with much labour and apparent satisfaction, as if to imply, "Ha, you see, I have got it at last!" I gave him up.

A full-grown nẏan ram stands about twelve hands or over, and is of a darkish-brown colour above and on the forequarters, shading into a paler hue on the belly and lower parts; he wears a great ruff of almost white hair on his neck, by which he may be distinguished at a long distance from the female, and has a ridiculous little apology for a tail (if anything pertaining to so noble a beast can be called ridiculous), about an inch in length; but what strikes one most is his build and legs, which remind one much more of those of a deer than a sheep, and no doubt account for his marvellous activity and swiftness of movement. His horns, though much shorter than those of the

Ovis Polii (which latter, I believe, is the smaller animal of the two), and without their graceful outward sweep, are tremendously massive. Starting upwards and backwards, after the usually accepted type of ram's horn, the horns of a full-grown nyan are from eighteen to twenty inches in circumference at the base, and curve downwards and forwards again till they form an almost complete circle; in fact, in one head that I possess both horns (though some inches are broken off at the tips, as is almost invariably the case with old rams) entirely cover the eyes and more than complete the circle.

The ewes are almost equal to the rams in stature, but are distinguishable from a long way off by the absence of the white ruff and the general dark colouring of the head and neck. They, too, carry horns, which, however, are not massive like those of the rams, but grow upwards and backwards, and are only some twenty inches in length. I have come across no animal the length of whose horns is so difficult to judge from a distance, even with the aid of a good glass, as those of the nyan ram. The "Badminton Library" attributes this fact to the colour of the horns, but I am inclined to think that it has something to do with the peculiar sweep of their curve.

The burhel (*Ovis nahura*) or, as they are called in Ladakh, "nāpoo," have a very wide range, extending from Zanskar and the borders of Baltistan on the west, right away to China on the east, where Bower, in his book "Across Thibet," tells us that he saw them. Southwards they are to be found within a few marches of Simla and other hill-stations on the southern slope of the main range of the Himalaya. More goat-like in their proclivities than the other Oves, they are seldom to be found far from precipitous ground, to which they betake themselves when alarmed or wounded. In build they differ greatly from the nẏan, being stouter and, so to speak, lower, with much shorter and thicker legs. In colour they are a bluish-grey, with a strongly marked medial line, and when lying on a slope of rock and shale, as is their wont, under the brilliant sun of these high regions, are most difficult to make out, unless they should chance to move. Their horns are most peculiar, and quite unlike those of any other animal. To describe their shape and curves so as to give an idea of their appearance is difficult, suffice it to say that they are smooth and rounded with a prominent ridge along the front, and an old horn has a curious appearance which can only be described as "creased." The horns, starting close together on the forehead, rise first upward and outward, then curve downward and outward, sweeping backward and upward to a point. As regards measurements, an average head would measure perhaps twenty-two inches in length, with a circumference at the base of eleven or twelve inches; but heads very much larger than this are

LEH.

CALIFORNIA

frequently obtained. As far as I have been able to observe personally, one is likely to meet with old rams in company with the ewes all through the year, as the males of this animal do not seem to separate entirely from the females during the summer months, as is the case with most mountain game. I consider an old ram burhel as difficult to bag as almost any of the Himalayan game that I have shot, as, unless hit in some vital part, he will go incredible distances, and a broken leg seems hardly to affect him at all. I have seen a ram, so badly wounded that he fell four times while still in sight, go right away over a high range of hills for some five miles before he lay down to die. But to return to my sport in Gya. The shikaris whom I sent out to prospect on the day of my arrival, reported both nẙan and nāpoo, and of course I went after the former first, as I was assured that I could get as many of the latter as I wished. The first day I went up Tubbuh, and saw, on the peak of a crag some 2,000 feet above me, a nāpoo gazing down into the valley below; but as there were here many tracks of nẙan, we did not go after him, but turned up a side nalah. About mid-day, as we were riding along the usual stony plain, we saw a reddish-coloured animal which came bounding down the slope on our left, and which, after going some little distance, stopped and commenced to feed. Salia said at first that he was a shāpoo, but the Ladakhi said, "No, a small nẙan."

I did not want a *small* nẙan, but never having seen one before, decided to stalk him, to see what he was like on closer acquaintance. Accordingly we rode up a steep but favourable nalah, and then climbed a low hill. As I cautiously peered over the crest the nẙan came up the other side, and we met one another face to face within one hundred yards.

I did not even put up my rifle, as I had been told that he was a small one, and after an instant's pause he fled down hill and across the valley. The shikaris now said, "Shoot! he is a good one," but it was too late. I fired at him as he fled, and, am sorry to say, wounded him, as there was blood on his tracks; but, though he was followed for some twenty miles, nearly down to the Indus, he was never recovered, so that I hope the wound was merely a graze, in fact, this was proved to be the case by the blood track ceasing soon afterwards, and the marks joining those of several ewes, whose company he evidently sought, which he would never have done had he been severely wounded. My feelings can be better imagined than described, as of course, being the first nẙan that I had ever seen, I had not known what to expect, and it would have been such an easy shot as we stood face to face! Nobody is more against shooting an animal with an insignificant head than myself; but I think that perhaps one should always shoot the *first* beast of any species that one sees, provided, of course, that it is a male, as one may never subsequently get a chance, and it does not fall to the luck of everyone to get a good head of a rare animal. The next chance that I got at nyan was in Kayma.

Saibra had been sent on early, and when we came up with him, had seen six rams a long way off. After some time we discovered them, lying down in the middle of a large open space, and far above us. To get near them seemed almost impossible; however, we ascertained the direction of the wind, and, as there were no clouds about, and no snow in the immediate neighbourhood, we hoped that it might hold steady during the stalk. This varying wind is the most trying factor in stalking in these regions, as anyone who has shot in Thibet well knows. If the day chance to be cloudy, or if snow or glaciers be near at hand, the wind is continually shifting to every point of the compass, and, as Ward says: "If the stalker feels a puff of wind on his back when within seven hundred or eight hundred yards of the game (nyan), he well knows that it is 'all up!'"

However, on this occasion the wind was good enough to keep steady. We climbed about one hundred feet to a small ridge above the plateau where we had seen the nyan and peeped over. There they were, all lying down on their sides in the sun, but about two hundred yards away, and, excited as I was, I refused to risk a shot at this distance. By crawling flat on our faces, Salia managed to gain about fifty yards, and there we lay watching the rams and waiting for them to get up. I had plenty of time to observe them through my glasses, but could not form the vaguest idea as to the length of their horns; however, I could make out that only one of them had a decided white ruff on his neck. After lying here for what seemed to me an age, but which must have been in reality about half an hour, a ram at last rose to his feet; he was not the one with the ruff, but Salia whispered, "Fire! he is a good one." Mindful of my last adventure, and thinking that if I did fire the big one would jump up and give me a shot, I took steady aim and pulled the trigger. Down fell the nẏan, dead as a door-nail; but the others, with what seemed one bound, sprang up and topped a ridge. I fired my other barrel at a big one and saw him falter, but he went on. Rushing down, full of joy at having shot my first nẏan, I found that he had a head—well, too small to mention. I nearly wept.

Some hours afterwards we recovered the big one, but even his head was under thirty inches, and I vowed, that having shot one nẏan, I would hereafter fire at nothing but a really big head. The meat was excellent to eat, and the camp rejoiced, and we all returned with severe neuralgic headaches, the result of the unaccustomed exertion at these heights. Now as to my hunting of the nāpoo, or burhel, in Gya.

The first day that I went out we had seen many tracks in Tubbuh, and, on a rock some thousands of

THE BRITISH JOINT-COMMISSIONER'S HOUSE AT LEH.

feet above us, a single ram had, as already described, appeared against the sky-line, standing motionless as he gazed down into the valley; he was accompanied by three ewes and a lamb. As, at that time we were intent on nyan, we let him be, and on the following day saw him again near the same spot; this time we also espied a large flock of nāpoo upon a precipitous crag on the other side of the valley. These latter, however, were a long way off, and being far above us, and on a slope of bluish-coloured shale, it was impossible to make out through the glass whether there were any big rams amongst them or not; accordingly, as it was now late in the evening, we left them. Two days later, after a lazy morning in camp, I had taken my shot-gun in the afternoon, and had been up a side nalah, in quest of hares and snow-pigeons, when, as I was returning homewards, I suddenly espied five nāpoo grazing on the mountain slope immediately above me, and on the same side of the valley as the camp. Hastily we got out of sight, and giving Ullia my pony, I told him to gallop off to camp, and send Salia and my rifle. Before long they arrived, and, as by this time it was getting dark, we began a hasty stalk straight up the hill towards the nāpoo who were immediately above us, taking advantage of the cover afforded by a little watercourse which led up towards them. At length, panting for breath, I cautiously raised my head, and was at the same moment observed by the nāpoo. The only ram amongst them was standing facing me and about one hundred and fifty yards away, but I had no time to consider and fired, missing him clean. As he rushed down the ridge, he showed up black against the sunset sky, and I let him have the second barrel. Kicking up a cloud of dust, he fell prostrate; we went after him, scrambling along as best we might, but when we were nearly within shot he was up and off again, not, however, before we had made out that he carried a good head. There was nothing for it, as it was by this time almost dark, but to let him go on, watching him through the glasses. Three times he stumbled and fell, and making sure that he would lie down to die a short way farther on, I sent Ullia to fetch him the following morning. Fetch him he did, but not until he had tracked him for some ten miles, and when he did come up, he found the carcase being devoured by two black wolves (*Canis Laniger*), of which there were several in this district. The nāpoo's head was a nice one, the horns being twenty-four inches long, and ten inches in circumference at the base.

The following day, early in the morning, I sent on the peasant from Gya with Saibra to scale the mountain opposite my camp and look out for nāpoo, and after breakfast followed myself with Salia and Ramzahn. This mountain consisted of a spur dividing two side ravines, and with a face of shale towards the camp, which admitted of my riding. Near the base of this slope was a curious funnel-shaped and deep pit, with almost perpendicular sides. This, the natives told me, was a wolf-trap, and was baited with a lamb, when the flock was folded in the vicinity. This unfortunate lamb naturally bleats loudly on finding himself alone in the dark at the bottom of the pit, and the wolf's attentions are devoted to him instead of the main flock. Once in he cannot get out again, and though he has probably enjoyed a good supper, Nemesis arrives next morning in the shape of huge rock, or possibly an antiquated muzzle-loader.

But to resume. After a longish pull we reached the top of the mountain opposite the camp, and here Saibra met us with the welcome news that he had seen a large flock of nāpoo feeding on the eastern side. The ground here consists of precipitous rocks at the top, with the usual steep stone slopes below. Advancing cautiously we soon made out a flock of about thirty nāpoo far below us; some were feeding on the scanty herbage, whilst others slept or rested on their sides, with their legs stretched out at full length. Amongst them were four or five good rams, but it was out of the question to fire at them from where I was, as they were some four hundred yards away, and directly below me. Accordingly, taking advantage of a ridge of rocks that ran vertically down the hillside, we clambered down, and having reached a point that we judged must be almost opposite to them, we peeped over. At that moment the wind changed, and blew from us straight towards them; in an instant they were all in full flight. It is incredible with what alacrity these animals, apparently stretched out fast asleep one moment,

"WE CLAMBERED DOWN ... AND PEEPED OVER."

will be galloping away with the rest of the flock a second afterwards. I ought not to have fired, but I was anxious to get a head, so putting up my sight for three hundred yards (they were far below me and going straight away), so as to be well ahead of the animal I aimed at, I fired right and left at two rams which were bringing up the rear of the flock. Both bullets told, one ram separating from the rest, while the other went on slowly, and evidently in distress. It was a lucky shot, but scarcely, I am afraid, to be commended as a sporting one. Almost immediately after I had fired, the curious effect of the atmosphere at these heights was well shown, as, though under ordinary conditions the flock should have been easily visible, being on open ground and only some five hundred yards away, yet they literally disappeared in the trembling heat-haze on the shale slope ; the remarkable sympathy in colour between the animal and the ground of course assisting in this.

The horns of the rams measured twenty-two and twenty-three inches respectively ; but the second one was not secured until he finally sank exhausted on a snow slope at about 18,000 feet some six miles away from where he was shot. Satisfied with my sport in the Gya Nalah, at any rate as far as the nāpoo were concerned, I set out on August 3rd to cross the Kiameri-La into the district of Tiri, which lies at the head of a valley running up to the south from the Indus. That day, however, I did not cross the Pass, but encamped at the head of Kayma, where there is a fine semicircle of parti-coloured mountains topped with snow. I scaled a high hill in the middle of this amphitheatre, which makes an admirable post of observation, but though we kept a sharp look-out all day, and sent watchers in two opposite directions, we saw neither nāpoo nor nÿan. The camp was here pitched in a pleasant valley, which was carpeted with the turf that grew on both sides of the stream, and where there was plenty of brushwood for firing—an agreeable surprise amongst the stony hills at this elevation. Amongst the wild flowers that grow here, I noticed a white dandelion, which was in great profusion, a large yellow fumitory, and a blue monk's-hood.

The following morning (August 4th) we crossed the Kiameri-La, a very easy Pass, which is probably between 16,000 and 17,000 feet high. On reaching the top, one has a good view of the district of Tiri, with a snow-clad spur on the right or southern side, and some precipitous mountains, that shut in the valley, to the north, towards the Indus. These latter hills are very brilliant in colouring, a crimson one with a stripe of slate-blue fading into violet and green mixed being specially effective. We had not gone far on the opposite side before Ullia espied ten nÿan rams across the valley, a very long way off. The Ladakhis declared that they were Kyang (wild asses), of which there are many hereabout; but I was positive that they were nÿan, as I could see their horns through my glasses, and asses have not horns! So we plunged hastily into the nalah and encamped there.

After a short time I ascended the gravelly down

to where we had seen the nyan, and soon made them out in a good position for a stalk; but, after scanning them through the telescope, and being sure that none of them had horns much over thirty inches, I remembered my determination of "nothing but big ones in future," and desisted from the chase. From this camp in the evening I espied a wolf, but he kept carefully at a distance of at least a quarter of a mile, and I could not get a shot at him.

CHAPTER VII.

WE had now fairly entered Rupshu, a country the description of which had always had a fascination for me. It is the highest inhabited country in the world, and "inhabited" means, in this case, by nomadic dwellers in tents, as, with the exception of the villages of Hanlé (14,276 feet) and Karzok (14,960 feet), both of which places consist of a Gonpa, or Monastery, with a few huts collected round the base of the spur on which this is built, these vast wastes can claim no settled dwelling-place. Rupshu proper lies to the south of the Indus, and consists of a series of uplands and valleys, which are nowhere lower than 14,000 feet above the sea-level. These are interspersed between, and traversed by, confused groups of mountains, that for the most part rise to a height of something over 20,000 feet, and appear to have no particular watershed, though the natural tendency of the whole district would be towards the Indus.

In many cases these valleys drain into the large brackish lakes, such as the Tso-Kar and Tso-

GROUP OF YAKS, LEH.

A SUMMER IN HIGH ASIA.

Moriri, which have no visible outlet, and are a peculiar feature of the country. The general appearance is one of vast stony plains, devoid of any but the scantiest vegetation, surrounded by rounded downs or hilltops, whose slopes are composed of shale or detritus, above which rise precipices and snowy peaks, while there are a few small glaciers in places, in the hollows of these hills. The perpetual snow-line in these regions is somewhere about 20,000 feet—in fact, the leading characteristic of these exposed highlands is the absence of any sign of moisture. To this add a burning sun by day, and a dry, biting atmosphere which seems to shrivel the skin, and which is intensified by a gale of freezing wind which always springs up about midday and blows till sunset, and you have a fair idea of Rupshu and its climate during the summer months. It freezes every night throughout the year. From this description one would imagine that a more bleak and inhospitable country could not exist, but, curiously enough, such is not the case.

There is one feature that particularly struck me. On the plains of India, the deserts of Africa and other barren regions, the glaring midday light seems to take all the colour out of the landscape, and reduce it to a study in strong black and white, but here such is not the case. As the sun gets higher the fantastic colouring seems to become intensified, as anyone who can recall a midday scene in Rupshu, with the brilliant blue of some salt lake in the foreground, surrounded by hills of every shade of red, yellow, and other colours, backed by the glittering snows against an azure sky, will remember. Also, by the side of any fresh water will be found the most vivid of bright green turf, and this is often carpeted with brilliant wild flowers, even though it may be but a yard or two in width, and a sight like this, after travelling for many weary hours across desolate wastes, loses nothing by the contrast. Even the stony plains are not devoid of colour, as the bits of rock and pebbles are of every imaginable hue, and frequently powdered with glittering mica, and might almost be said to rival in colouring the flowers of more fertile countries. The chief fascination of these regions, however, and one which seems to affect even the most prosaic of mortals, is the sense of freedom and boundless space which one experiences as one gazes on these vast solitudes of hilltop and plain; a sort of feeling, as one looks round, knowing that there is probably no human being except one's own camp for many (it may be hundreds) of miles in any direction, and that the country, so to speak, belongs to oneself to go where and how one likes, which once experienced is never forgotten.

The intensely dry and rarefied atmosphere of these high regions is often found extremely trying by those who are not accustomed to it, and a sickness is experienced which usually takes the form of intense headache or neuralgia, and giddiness, with occasional vomiting, and even bleeding at the nose and ears. This is scarcely to be wondered at when the fact is taken into consideration that the atmospheric pressure at a height of 14,000 feet is, roughly speaking, one-half of what it is at sea-level. The oxygen is therefore greatly reduced, with the effect of making respiration a much more difficult matter. It is curious to observe here, how the slightest upward incline seems to be as "pumping" as a steep climb would be at a lower elevation. This feeling is of course increased by any exertion, such as running, and the heart begins to beat at a tremendous pace; in fact, I have felt the heart-beats of a pony that I have been riding, just as one feels the throbbings of the engines on board an ocean steamer. Never shall I forget climbing up a steepish bank at an elevation of perhaps 19,000 feet, and immediately afterwards trying to light my pipe; the inhalation caused me to feel as if (in schoolboy phrase) someone had "taken my wind" violently. One soon learns to adopt a system of respiration, which I found universal amongst the natives of these regions, of taking a much longer and deeper breath than is our ordinary habit. Remedies suggested for this discomfort are chlorate of potash and coca; but I think that one gets accustomed to the rarefied atmosphere in a short time, and feels no ill effect, as long as no extra exertion is necessary, though the experiences of individuals seem to vary greatly. Amongst my camp I was lucky in finding but few who suffered for long, as most of them speedily got acclimatised, though curiously enough the Kashmiri shikaris, and notably Salia, suffered much at times, particularly from pains in the head. According to Drew, the best authority on this country, the area of Rupshu is 4,000 square miles, and there are but five hundred indigenous inhabitants. These inhabitants, Chang-Pa as they are called, do not seem to feel the climate much, but will never undertake any violent exercise such as carrying a coolie's load, all the porterage being performed by yāks, ponies, or sheep. These Chang-Pa are a curious people. They live in tents made of skins, which are about twelve or fourteen feet long, eight wide, and not more than about four feet high. These tents are open at the top to admit of the escape of the smoke from the fire inside, and also, let us hope, of ventilation; they are also made more roomy, and at the same time fortified against the diurnal visitation of the Ladakhi gale, by ropes fastened to them at intervals, and pulled taut by means of small poles (what the interior of these habitations may be like I cannot say, as I could never summon up the courage to enter one of them). They are ornamented, as is the case with most dwellings in this country of Lamas, with rag banners and yāks' tails on long poles. The Chang-Pa seem to be a hardy, cheery race, rather smaller in stature than the Ladakhis, but with the same Mongol-features (perhaps a trifle

more emphasised), short pig-tails, and generally decaying-from-dirt appearance.

When supplying the traveller with yāks for transport, goats for milk, and sheep for food, they will accompany him for many stages of his journey, till he reaches the next camp, where he can obtain what he requires; their wives, children, and dogs accompany them, cheerfully sleeping in the open at night time, and for ever singing their curious plaintive little song. Travelling in this way one learns to appreciate the patriarchal mode of progression with one's flocks and herds!

The Chang-Pa's only worldly wealth seems to lie in their flocks of thousands of sheep and goats, of which they sell the "pushm," or under-coat of wool, with which Nature endows all animals at these elevations to protect them against the severity of the cold. This wool trade, with the transport which they supply to travellers and merchants between China and Leh, seems to be their only source of income. That they are not without money was proved to me on one occasion, when, having run short of rupees (my fresh supply not having arrived from Leh), my guide, Ramzahn, borrowed somewhat extensively from the head man of one of these camps. This chief was quite surprised and pleased to receive a small interest on his loan a day or two later, and told me at first that I had made some mistake; civilisation has not yet spoilt the natives of these parts! During the winter the Chang-Pa take their flocks and yāks down to the valley of the Indus, to the grazing-grounds near Nyuma and Dora, and I found out by conversation that it is a fact that they look upon Leh as a place that can only be visited in the coldest weather, and, even then, not without some danger of succumbing to the heat, while, as for Kashmir, they think that anyone who can stand its torrid climate must be a very salamander! Such is the country and people of the district which I was going to visit in the pursuit of nẏan and goa.

On August 5th we left the Tiri Nalah, and, climbing up to the high ground where we had seen the nẏan on the previous day, we found ourselves upon a table-land, from whence a fine view was obtainable down towards the Indus, while across the valley of the latter river and in the distance, a prominent object was the range which is crossed by the Thatoo-La on the way to the Pangong Lake and Changchenmo. The sun was topping the eastern hills as we emerged on to the plateau, and, standing on an isolated knoll, I saw an animal that was strange to me then, though he was to become almost too familiar in the future. Like a statue he stood there motionless, gazing over the stony plain towards the rising sun. He was a kyang, that strange animal that, half horse, half ass, but not quite like either, inhabits the highlands of these regions sometimes in twos and threes, and sometimes, as I have heard (though I never saw more than about fifty together) in vast droves. The kyang (*Equus hemionus*) is in shape and size more like a zebra than either a horse or donkey, and is in colour a rich chestnut, with a dark dorsal stripe that extends from the withers to the tail, the latter being of some length, reaching to the hocks. The lower part of the body, and the inside of the legs, is pure white, and the medial line, or division between the colours of the upper and lower parts, is very marked; so much so, indeed, that at some distance, and on a plain that is quivering in the midday sunlight, one observes what seems to be the upper half of an animal without any corresponding lower half. These kyang are literally the nightmare (or should one say "mares"?) of the sportsman in Thibet, as they are almost always to be found in places where dwell nÿan and goa, and, being, I should say, the most inquisitive brutes in existence, they no sooner observe the ardent stalker crawling on his face across the stones towards the coveted game, than one of them is sure to trot up to see what on earth is going on. As soon as he has ascertained that it is some lunatic who is apparently amusing himself in this strange way, the kyang calls the rest of the herd, who, after satisfying their curiosity by a brief survey, gallop away snorting and kicking, and of course putting every animal in the neighbourhood on the alert. I have seen them come quite close to the camp (their curiosity being apparently insatiable) when it has been pitched in some unusual locality, and have very often been urged to shoot them by the Chang-Pa and by my servants, but of that more anon. On foot I found that it was difficult to approach the kyang, but if mounted they seemed to be much interested, and would allow one to approach quite close. On one occasion I thought, being mounted on a much better native pony than usual, that I would try and gallop a small herd of some four or five of them, and accordingly started, as I imagined, in pursuit; what was my surprise, therefore, when I found that they, in their turn, were galloping straight towards me; and, just as a collision seemed imminent, and I was wondering what would happen next, they wheeled in perfect order, as if they had been drilled, in "sections outward," allowing me to pass through them somewhat surprised! Another of the kyang's amiable tricks is to come at night and decoy away your ponies, should these latter not be securely hobbled, with the result that, when you get up early in the morning, prepared to make a long march, you find no baggage animals, and have to waste a day in camp whilst these are being retrieved, kicking your heels, and blessing the kyang.

But to return to my journey. On this high ground I noticed several wild flowers that were quite unknown to me, more especially a plant that formed a very closely-growing round tuft, and which I frequently observed on subsequent occasions. This tuft was generally some six or eight inches in diameter, and rose at the centre, perhaps some four inches from the ground; the fibres were so closely interlaced that it was difficult to break one of these tufts in half, and they were covered with pretty little starlike white blossoms. These tufts seem to be the favourite resort of a small animal like a tail-less rat, some eight inches in length, which seems to burrow into, and live beneath, them. I caught one of these little beasts, and identified it as *Lagomys Ladakensis* (the Ladakh Pika, Sterndale). After leaving the high ground we crossed a valley and ascended the other side, and on this slope we encountered ground such as I never saw, at any rate to the same extent, anywhere else, though I fancy that it must be in a similar soil to this that the disappearing rivers, that I so frequently noticed in Baltistan, lose themselves. (In that country it was not unusual to see a considerable stream vanish from sight in the loose detritus, sometimes to reappear equally suddenly some way farther on, but not infrequently to be no more seen.) To look at, this ground presented the appearance of the ordinary shale slope, but for some miles it was in consistency like a quicksand, into which the ponies sank up to their hocks, while the foot-passengers fared but little better; a state of things which was evidently caused by the rapidly-melting snow-fields immediately above the loose shale. After struggling through this slough of despond we arrived on a plain, said to be a favourite haunt of goa, but on this occasion we saw none here.

Some miles farther on we came upon a very striking scene. The plateau on which we were ends somewhat abruptly, and, far below us, to the south-east, stretched the Tso-Kar, or "Nimak-Talao" (salt-lake), by which latter name it seems to be more generally known in these parts, the Thog-Ji Chenmo of Moorcroft. The waters of this lake, of a brilliant hue, are in outline somewhat like a trefoil, and surrounded by shores that

"WE CAME UPON A VERY STRIKING SCENE."

glisten with the brilliant white of salt and natron deposits. Surrounding it is a perfect amphitheatre of mountains of the usual yellow and red tints, backed by lofty snows, some of them at a great distance. As we were halted here, waiting for our baggage-animals to arrive, a herd of some hundreds of sheep and goats approached us, driven by the Chang-Pa herdsmen and herdswomen. Not long afterwards we heard wild yells and saw a wolf carrying off a kid, so to speak, beneath our very noses; a bold proceeding at midday! To jump on to our ponies was the work of a moment for Salia

CHORTEN IN THE CITY OF LEH.

CALIFORNIA

A SUMMER IN HIGH ASIA.

and myself, and off we started in hot pursuit. After he had gone about a quarter of a mile, the wolf noticed us following him, and, dropping the kid, went and sat down on his haunches some way farther on. In vain did we try to stalk the wary brute, he always kept just out of shot, so I eventually returned and concealed myself behind a boulder near the carcase of the kid (which he had half eaten as he carried it in his mouth, running away as he was at the time!) in the hope that he would return for it. It was no good, he was far too cunning to come back, and we never saw him again. That night we encamped in an adjacent ravine, in the hopes of seeing goa, but only does showed themselves, and the one object of interest was a lot of kyang who came down and closely inspected the camp.

On the following day we went up on to the plateau again, and after sighting some nyan ewes and lambs (one of the former was lame, surely no "sportsman" had fired at and wounded her), and a few doe goa, we at length saw a solitary buck gazelle. We endeavoured to stalk him, but he had seen us, and though after some hours' work I got a shot at him at about three hundred yards, I was scarcely surprised when I missed him clean, as this little animal stands only some eighteen inches high. On the morrow (August 7th) we left the higher ground, and made for a camping place on the edge of the Nimak-Talao, called Thugji. On the way we had to cross the mouth of a wide plain, which comes down from a valley in the mountains to the eastwards. This district rejoices in the name of Puttatuktuk, and is the locality to which every sportsman who is in these parts, and who wants to shoot a goa, is conducted by his shikaris. There is, to my knowledge, one herd of gazelle on this plain, and, also to my knowledge, this herd had been fired upon by at least four separate sportsmen during the season, before my arrival, so that they were becoming knowing in their generation; however, we hoped for the best.

I had sent on to Saibra to prospect, and followed ahead of the yāks a little later. As we crossed the plain we saw him on an isolated hillock, that stands conveniently in the middle of it, beckoning to us to come to him. I sent back to stop the yāks, and when we reached him he told us that he had seen a herd of goa, *the* herd, and that they had lain down in a small depression in the plain, which he pointed out to us. I was resolved to be extra painstaking in the stalking of these animals, as the account I had received of the hunting of them, from a friend who had pursued them in this very spot earlier in the season, was as follows:—

"At last you see a herd of little brown specks, and are told that these are goa. You proceed to crawl on your face for miles across an open plain, composed of the sharpest-pointed stones imaginable.

until you come to within about two hundred yards of the aforesaid specks; nearer than this you cannot get. You then select the one that is darkest in colour—this you believe to be the big buck (to distinguish their horns at this distance is impossible)—and fire, continuing to pump lead into the herd as long as they are within sight, with or without success."

This account, though perhaps a little exaggerated, certainly gives one a good idea of the difficulties of pursuing this little animal, more especially when the object of one's hunt is the Puttatuktuk herd, and I must confess that the Thibetan gazelle gave me far more trouble to obtain than any other of the game in these parts, not excepting the nyan; though, from what I have been told, and, indeed, have seen myself, given favourable ground, this little animal offers an occasional easy shot, and, from his habit of stopping after he has gone a short distance, frequently affords an opportunity of a second one if you follow him up.

Of such, however, are not the goa of Puttatuktuk, and, after fulfilling my friend's programme almost to the very letter, I found myself obliged to seek the camp empty-handed, though my shikaris declared that one buck was wounded. As we did not retrieve him, I hope that this was not the case, though he certainly did turn away from the herd, which is usually a sign of the bullet having told.

A SUMMER IN HIGH ASIA.

Bower says, in his book "Across Thibet": "Lots of gazelle (goa) were to be seen about; they are infinitely more knowing than either antelope or yāk, and in the most out-of-the-way parts of Thibet promptly made off on seeing the caravan as if they were accustomed to being shot at regularly." Again: "Shooting them is not nearly such easy work as shooting antelope."

Our camp was pitched on the eastern side of

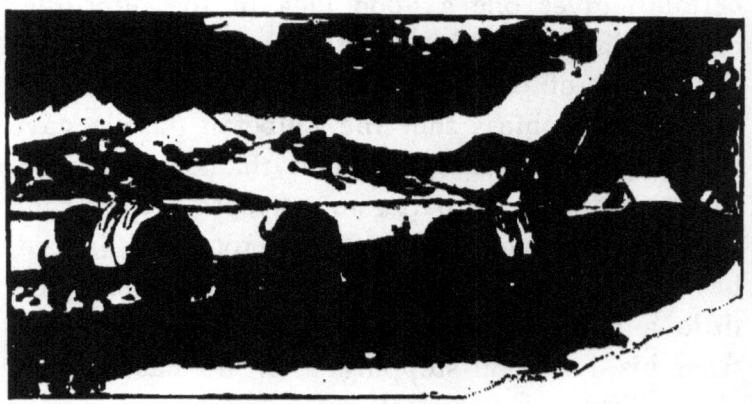

CAMP AT THE TSO-KAR—YĀKS FEEDING.

the lake, at the foot of some brightly-coloured spurs. The ground between us and the open water is covered with a crust of white saline deposit some half a mile in breadth, and this is intersected by curious chasms and holes, some of them of a considerable depth, which makes it difficult to traverse. Round the outer edge of this deposit is a stretch of boggy turf, brilliantly green and covered with wild flowers, whilst the shores

THE STATE DISPENSARY IN LEH.

appear to be a favourite breeding-ground of the "Brahminy" duck (*Casarca rutila*), the bar-headed goose (*Anser indicus*), and innumerable terns and gulls. This fact was noticed by Moorcroft, and chronicled by him in his account of his travels in these parts, now some seventy years ago.

The following day was a hard-working one, and the account of it I had best take from my diary:—

"We started at 9.30 A.M. up the nalah behind camp. It looked a fairly easy climb from below, but was in fact one of the worst that I have attempted. Not very steep, but all loose detritus, which gave way at every step. This was the sort of mountain that, if you were to start half-way up it to go to the top, for every step that you went up you would slip down two, and eventually find yourself at the bottom. However, the pony that I was riding (hardly bigger than a Shetland) struggled bravely on, and after two-and-a-half hours' climb under a hot sun, we found ourselves at the summit. Before us and on our left hand was a large undulating plain, and on our right a ridge of snow-covered hills. Here we saw nothing living save two or three kyang with a foal. These did not seem to pay us much attention, though they were doubtless surprised at seeing human beings up here. An hour or two later we made out, through the telescope, six whitish specks, about two miles away on a ridge, and decided that they were nyan. Starting off as fast as we could, we crossed two intervening valleys and ridges and caught sight of them again, but at the same time saw an animal also going in their direction, which turned out to be a large wolf; he had got a long start of us, and, if he was bent on stalking the same flock of nyan, small chance was there for us. However, on seeing us, he slunk away to the right, and not long afterwards, cautiously peering over a ridge, we saw the six nyan immediately below us; we made a successful stalk, and arrived within fifty yards of them, but to my disgust there was nothing carrying horns of even thirty inches, so we showed ourselves, and watched them gallop away across the ridge in front towards the Indus Valley. Almost immediately afterwards we saw another wolf, that had apparently come from the opposite direction, slinking away. This particular flock of nyan seemed to be having a rather bad time of it. It was now 5 P.M., and we had more than ten miles to go to get back to camp, where we arrived at 7.30 P.M., all of us pretty well done up."

The next day was spent in an ineffectual attempt to get a shot at the Puttatuktuk goa. On the morrow (August 10th) we followed the road southwards along the lake, and then turned to the east up the Polakonka Pass, as I had heard of a flock of nyan there, out of which one had been shot a short time previously. The road was easy, rising gradually between snow-covered hills till the top is reached, 16,300 feet above the sea-level; here we camped, just under the summit, on some good turf by the side of a stream. The following day we started up the range to the south in search of nyan, as it was here that I had heard that there were some good ones. A fairly easy slope took us up to the snow-line, which was, I suppose, at that time at about 18,000 feet, and here we stopped for some time to prospect. Seeing nothing, we began to work westwards along the ridge. Soon afterwards Salia was in such pain from mountain sickness and neuralgia in the head that I sent him back to camp.

A SUMMER IN HIGH ASIA.

It was near here that Moorcroft and his party, or rather his companion Trebeck, suffered so severely from the same cause some seventy years before, and which he describes so quaintly but truly: "The whole party suffered much inconvenience from difficulty of breathing. This sensation in mountainous countries is not, perhaps, exactly what is understood by similar difficulty in the plains; it may be best defined a frequent inclination, and, at the same time, a sense of inability, to sigh."

After traversing the snow for about a mile, and keeping a sharp look-out on to the slopes below, we at length saw a herd of seven nyan in a corrie below us. At this moment an opportune snowstorm came on, and, taking advantage of it, we quickly dropped down the boulder-strewn precipice towards the sheep. The shower soon passed, and, when it cleared, we found ourselves within two hundred yards of the nyan. Eagerly I scanned their heads, but, argue to myself as I would, I could not imagine any horns much over thirty inches. Much disappointed, I came out from beyond my rock and showed myself in the open, and now the most annoying thing happened; the nyan looked at me for several seconds, and I had actually to wave my pocket-handkerchief before they made off, and then proceed in a leisurely way across a snow-slope in full view. Would they have done this if they had been forty inches? It really almost looked as if they were aware that they were too small to be fired at. Scrambling down the hillside was the very—well, was exceedingly steep, and the wind was so high that I found it hard to keep my Etna alight to cook my mid-day cup of Bovril. As I neared my camp, I was astonished to observe some additional tents pitched, and found that H. of the Goorkhas, whom I had met in India some years before, had arrived and joined camp. The pleasure of meeting a fellow white man can only be appreciated by one who has only had natives to speak to for some weeks, or, it may be, months, and our dinner that night was a merry one. We agreed that, as our roads lay in the same direction, we would proceed together.

CHAPTER VIII.

The following day we descended the Polakonka Pass (H. having to leave most of his camp behind until his ponies, which had been enticed away during the night by the kyang, had been recaptured) and arrived at Puga. This encampment is situated in a basin of green turf, watered by a stream, and has a small population, who work the sulphur and borax, which they here dig out of the hillside, and after, as far as we could make out, boiling it in roughly-made cauldrons (Moorcroft says with a sort of suet), pack it in small bags, and send it down to India on the backs of sheep, each of which latter carries two bags slung panier-wise. Ramzahn told me that these sheep have the fat cut out of their flanks when alive (perhaps to make the afore-mentioned suet), so that they may be the better carriers; they certainly looked very thin! At Puga we halted for a day, and H. and I explored the hills to south in search of goa, but saw none. I climbed into a very narrow and high ravine to the westward, but though I made my way right up to a glacier, some five miles up it, saw nothing but some Nāpoo ewes. The next day we continued our way down the road that here runs through a narrow ravine till it reaches the Indus Valley; the mountains on either side are precipitous, and look as if made for Nāpoo. Here we were caught up by my post coolie from Leh, who brought not only letters and papers, but another proof of the Joint-Commissioner's thoughtfulness and kindness in the shape of a kilta full of potatoes. Amongst his many trophies of the chase H. had secured, alive, a young Thibetan lynx (*Felis Isabellinus*), in the vernacular termed Ee. It was a cub, little bigger than a cat, of a reddish colour, that showed darker spots in certain lights, and had tufted ears, and tremendously strong legs and paws; sometimes he was as playful as a kitten, but he used to get bored when marching, as he travelled chained on to the top of the baggage on a pony, which latter animal master Ee would occasionally surprise by digging his somewhat formidable claws into his neck as he went along. On the top of the Polakonka Pass the Ee was allowed to escape during a night march (these animals are nocturnal in their habits, and get very restless, like most carnivora, as soon as the sun sets), but was luckily retrieved, as the chain that was round his neck was seen by the man who had been sent to recover him (and who, listening by night, had been led to the spot by his cries) projecting from beneath the stone under which he had taken refuge. This Ee, which is a rare animal, is

A SUMMER IN HIGH ASIA.

at present, I believe, in the Calcutta Zoological Gardens. From our camp, near the junction of the Polakonka and Indus roads, we started next day, and soon reached the valley of the latter river, but how different to the same valley lower down! Here the river is a broad, and occasionally shallow, stream flowing between grassy flats, a strong contrast to the furious torrent that rages through the gloomy gorges of Baltistan! Up this valley we marched till we reached a camping-ground opposite the district of Nyuma Mud, where there is a village, and, unless eyes and glasses deceived us, a tree! This encamping-ground is used as a pasture by the Chang-Pa during the winter months, and following the river you may see the road to Lhassa and Chinese Thibet, that country so attractive, but alas, at present so inaccessible, to the British sportsman!

There is no harm in saying now, as it never came off, that H. and I had an idea of camping near the frontier and making a dash into Chinese Thibet, shooting our nyan and wild yāk and returning. A man had even been engaged who had promised to guide us to the forbidden land, and was to have met us at Nyuma; but I suppose that his courage failed him at the last moment, as he never turned up. There is an amusing story of an adventurous young officer who endeavoured to get into Chinese Thibet by various means, but had always been stopped by the frontier guards, and who was delighted when at last the inhabitants appeared to give in to his solicitations (and a liberal "backsheesh"). He proceeded to be slung across the Indus in a basket running on a rope; but when suspended in mid-air over the middle of the raging torrent, to his dismay the basket stopped, and he was only hauled back (to the Ladakh side) on promising not to make any more attempts to cross into Chinese Thibet, where, however, the "backsheesh" remained! The country that lies immediately to the east of the frontier must be a veritable sportsman's paradise for yāk, nẏan, &c. Indeed, the description given by Bower, who crossed it in the course of his adventurous journey, proves it to be so; and those plucky, or lucky, sportsmen who have got across the frontier have been rewarded. Baulked of our intended expedition into Chinese territory, H. and I took counsel what road to pursue. I was inclined to cross the Indus and take the northward track by the Thātoo-La, to the Pangong Lake and Changchenmo, in search of nẏan, and subsequently of antelope and a possible yāk. My plans were also influenced by the fact that Saibra and Ramzahn knew the nẏan ground about the Thātoo-La, and promised me sport, whereas the ground in the Hanlé direction, south of the Indus, was unknown to them.

However, H. had reliable information about the latter, which he was generous enough to impart to me. I have noticed that this is not always the case

ANEMOMETER AND METEOROLOGICAL STATION AT LEITH.

amongst sportsmen, who, when they have discovered good ground, will not divulge the fact to a soul. This may be necessary in some cases, such as the neighbourhood of a large cantonment where ground is soon shot out, but I cannot see why, in an ordinary case, if one is lucky enough to discover a really good place, and has finished with it oneself, one should not let the whole world know of it, of course telling one's own friends first, so that they

INDUS VALLEY AT NYUMA MUD.

may reap the advantage. I decided to accompany H., one reason being that, had I chosen the northern route, I should have had to own myself defeated by the goa, as it was extremely improbable that I should come across any of these animals north of the Indus. It was lucky for me that I came to this determination, as will afterwards be shown, and I subsequently heard that all the parties who visited the Thātoo-La ground during that season met with little or no success, whereas by following the southern route I was, as it turned out, to be well rewarded. The following day we remained encamped opposite Nyuma Mud, and about midday there arrived a somewhat imposing *cortège*, which also halted here, and pitched camp about a quarter of a mile away from us, the chief tent being a rather striking one of blue and white stripes with golden poles! We wondered who on earth it could be who was travelling in this swell fashion, and I shortly afterwards received a message to say that the Chagzōt had arrived and would be happy to call upon me during the afternoon. I of course replied that I should be only too delighted to receive him, though who the Chagzōt might be I hadn't the faintest idea. He came to visit me with a large retinue, and after the usual "dalis" (presents) had been exchanged and rupees touched, &c., we kept up a conversation of a necessarily intermittent character (as every sentence had to pass through two interpreters) for some little time. He appeared *en grande tenue;* but I am afraid that H. and myself, in our shirt-sleeves and sitting on my bed, cannot have impressed him much, though perhaps he imagined that ours was the English *costume de parade* in which to receive distinguished visitors. I discovered that the Chagzōt is a sort of head Lama who visits all the monasteries, where he collects the rents, &c., and that he was then on his way to the Hanlé Gonpa. He had been told by the Wazir of

A SUMMER IN HIGH ASIA.

Leh that he would probably meet me, and was to look after me, and was accordingly very civil, and as it afterwards turned out, very useful. The next day we started up the left bank of the Indus, and after going some three or four miles came across the Chagzōt, who had started early, and was now halted with his party for his morning meal. He courteously invited us to join him. It was a picturesque scene: the Thibetans were seated on the greensward near the river; the old man himself had a fine intelligent face, and was, of course, dressed all in red, with a hat that very much resembled in shape that worn by a Cardinal; his following were brilliantly arrayed in Chinese fashion, and the whole were grouped on carpets and saddles, surrounded by their bell-bedecked horses and mules, and with the broad Indus and the stony desert for a background. H.'s and my own European appearance seemed to strike quite a discordant note in the scene; but we were made very welcome and treated with the greatest courtesy. The old gentleman had the most charming manner, though we could not, of course, understand what he was saying, but we found an interpreter among his suite who could translate our Hindustani to him. We were offered dried mutton, apricots, and chang. The latter is the universal beverage of the country, and is a sort of barley beer. When good and clean, as it was on this occasion, its rather acid taste is not unpleasant on a hot day, but as usually imbibed by the

Thibetans, very thick and poured out of their not overclean vessels, is not very inviting, and looks like muddy barley-water. The following is the recipe for the manufacture of "chang," as given by Moorcroft: "The grain (barley) is boiled until it is soft, and then dried; to about ten pounds of this softened grain, three ounces of the dough used for wheat cakes, but dried and pounded, are added, and the mixture is put into a bag, and kept in a warm place until it ferments, which it does usually in two or three days. Equal measures of the prepared barley and cold water are put together in an earthen vessel, and after standing two days the fluid is strained off; a similar quantity of water is again added, and treated in the same manner, and the beverage is the liquor called 'chang.'"

The Chagzōt was the possessor of a small dog of the Lhassa breed, looking something like a skye terrier, which was evidently a great favourite, and was not forgotten during the repast. In the meantime our servants were regaled with tea by the Lama retinue. After this short halt we pursued our way, and soon afterwards, leaving the Indus Valley, crossed a low ridge into the nalah of the Hanlé River, which comes down from a range to the southwards. On the road we saw no living animal save the everlasting kyang, and eventually encamped on a stretch of green boggy turf, where there was some tamarisk and "japsang" for fuel. The mosquitoes in the middle of the day were terrible, but they fortunately retired to rest before the frost, which set in as soon as the sun set. From the climate at this elevation, I fancy that these mosquitoes must be of a similar breed to those encountered in far northern Europe during the summer. At this camp we were passed by the Chagzōt who was pushing on, and intended to reach Hanlé in one more march, instead of the two that we intended to make. The following day H. and I shot through the considerable stretch of brushwood by the side of the river, as we marched along, and made a varied bag, which included a large buzzard (shot for its skin), bar-headed geese, pigeons, and several hares, the three latter items being a very welcome addition to our somewhat straitened commissariat.

The next march took us to Hanlé, or Hang Lé, as it is sometimes spelt, and the only noteworthy incidents were our having to gallop, in one place, to higher ground, to avoid the mosquitoes that stung our hands and faces like stinging-nettles, and the chasing of an unknown species of duck in the river, which, however, escaped, though it did not take to flight, owing to the fact that we had not our guns with us at the moment, and found stones, though propelled with considerable accuracy by H., an inefficient substitute.

Hanlé consists of an imposing-looking monastery of the usual semi-fortified type, perched on a lofty spur above the river, with a small collection of hovels and churtens below it. The elevation of the village is 14,276 feet, and it is one of the highest permanent habitations in the world. There is one narrow field of barley or grim at the foot of the

FORTIFIED MONASTERY OF HANLÉ.

rocks on which the Gonpa is built; but, as it was not even in ear at this season (August), I should say that the chances of its ripening were of the most remote! To the south and west of Hanlé extends a considerable plain, watered by the river of the same name, and surrounded by low sandy hills and uplands, which are, in their turn, backed by snows. It is an out-of-the-way corner of the world, and enjoys about three months of summer, during which period a snow-storm is not impossible or even improbable; what the climate must be during the long winter months is too awful to contemplate. There are fish in the river, and on his return journey H. had some sport with them.

As soon as we had pitched our tents at Hanlé the Chagzōt, who had arrived on the previous day, sent us a present of a sheep, some pubboos (native boots of embroidered cloth of brilliant hues, with skin soles), and, most welcome gift of all, some fresh vegetables, in the shape of small turnips; I don't know whence these latter were obtained. He also sent me a very old shikari, who had instructions to take me to good ground for nyan, and whose son accompanied H. This old man's name was Chering Doorji, he had been employed by many "Sahibs" who had visited these parts in days gone by, and had stories without end to tell about them. He knew every inch of the surrounding country, and, having been told to show me good sport by his spiritual chief, the Chagzōt, did so in a very short time, as will be seen. This fact was all the more fortunate for me, as, had I been without an introduction of the sort, the Thibetans would have been far too lazy to have shown me sport of their own accord, even had they been inclined to do so, and I might have searched the barren hills for days, or even weeks, without discovering the whereabouts of big rams, or, more likely still, have had to return without having seen one at all. However, time was no object, and I was determined to have a shot at a big one somehow before leaving. This night being the last that H. and I would spend together, we had a great feast, and, over a bumper of champagne, vowed that we would shoot a forty-inch nyan or perish in the attempt. In case the reader should be surprised at our possession of such a luxury as champagne, it may be as well to explain that H. had sent to the one shop in Leh for, amongst other things, a bottle of brandy, as he had run short, and wanted it for medicinal purposes. The coolie returned with a bottle of champagne, and the following explanation from the Hindu shopkeeper. "Sahib, I have *no* brandy, *so* I send a bottle of champagne!"

On the following morning (August 20th) H. and I parted, he setting out to the southwards for the Koyul Nalah, whilst I was to cross the river, and to hunt along the foot of the range of hills which rises to the eastwards, dividing the latter valley from that of the Hanlé River. Fresh snow had fallen during the night, which might drive the nyan down to lower grounds, so I started with great expectations. Our way led across, or rather through, the river, and then over

A SUMMER IN HIGH ASIA.

the plain in a northerly direction; I skirted the foot-hills, and, besides many kyang, saw a flock of eight nyan, which, after a careful and somewhat arduous stalk, was found to contain only two small rams, and we also saw many fresh tracks of goa, though the animals themselves were invisible. We were told that the rocks above were a favourite haunt of nāpoo, and, indeed, we saw a flock of the latter animal late in the evening, when daylight was failing.

The camp was pitched on the margin of a little stream that suddenly appears, coming out of the shingle, and on turf surrounded by a fair amount of brushwood for fuel. It was situated immediately below the lowest of the foot-hills. That night (August 20th) there was a tremendous hailstorm and a gale of wind which culminated in a regular tempest, accompanied by thunder and lightning, while snow fell to within a quarter of a mile of the tents—a pleasant midsummer experience! The following day was *the* red-letter day of my trip. I had sent off Saibra early, with a Ladakhi, along the range northward, whilst Ullia and Ramzahn had started southward along the ground that we had traversed the previous day. About eight o'clock I started off with Salia and Chering Doorji, and we determined to follow the latter party. We had not gone far when we observed them some way above us, and they eventually stopped and made signals to us to come up and join them. We were about to set off, when we saw a breathless coolie coming up from the camp, who said that Saibra had sent to say that he had seen four large nyan rams. For a moment I was undecided; we knew what to expect in one direction, and in the other it might be only a few burhel or nyan ewes, so my mind was soon made up, and, mounting our ponies, Salia and I set off at a gallop along the low, many-coloured hills of shingle towards Saibra, leaving Ullia still waving frantically from a hill-top. After going about a mile, we caught up the Ladakhi who had been sent back to camp by Saibra, and who, having delivered his message, was about to rejoin him. This Ladakhi, too, had seen the nyan, and said that they were all very big rams.

At last my chance had come! After many weary stalks and disappointments, all of them at an altitude of well over 15,000 feet, and just as I began to think that no nyan existed that carried a head of much over thirty inches, I was at length to be rewarded. As we galloped along, I pictured to myself how the first two barrels might drop two big rams, right and left, while, hastily reloading, I should get a chance at the remaining two (and of course hit them) as they vanished over the opposite slope. It struck me, however, that in the meantime they might have moved off before we could get there, as they are quick and restless feeders, and that when we came up to Saibra he would tell us that they were gone, and "Oh, Sahib, why were you not here about half-an-hour ago, you would have had a splendid shot," &c. Such a thought did not exactly lend me wings, but induced me to kick my steed along harder than ever. At last we saw Saibra, running along the hillside, and, thank goodness, looking intently below him, so that the quarry were evidently still in sight. We sprang off our ponies, and, starting them quickly in the opposite direction, sent them off loose, but out of sight. When we had crept up to Saibra, he told us that the rams had been resting close to him, but had just moved away. Of course! However, a few minutes later four red specks appeared, far below us. To change the shooting-boots that I was wearing for felt-soled "Chaplis," was the work of a minute, and then Salia, Saibra, and self started off in pursuit, telling the Ladakhis, who had by this time come up, and who naturally wanted to come with us and see the fun, to stop where they were, catch the ponies, and keep out of sight. Wriggling down the slope on our faces, we reached a friendly ravine which ran straight down hill.

There was no time to be lost, as the rams were feeding quickly onwards. Down this nalah, which was some ten feet in depth, we ran as fast as we could without making a noise, and at last cautiously peered over the edge. There were the rams, still below us and about half a mile away. Salia now performed the finest bit of stalking that I have ever seen (I must give him all the credit for it, as I should never have attempted it myself). Seeing that the nyan were feeding away from us, he told us to crouch as low as we could and follow him; then, climbing out of the ravine, we rushed across the open Maidan for quite three hundred yards, in full view of the nyan, to the shelter of a big rock, where we lay panting, having gained this distance upon them. It was a risky manœuvre to attempt; but it was a case of shot or no shot. Here we lay and observed them. I anxiously scanned them through my glasses, half expecting to experience the disappointing feeling to which I was becoming accustomed of seeing nothing over thirty inches; but, this time, though the length of their horns is so deceptive, I could see in a moment how different they looked to any rams that I had seen previously, and was sure that they all carried heads of over thirty-eight inches, and two of them, I should say, of over forty. But now a new danger presented itself; the wind, more than usually shifty, owing, I suppose, to the fresh snow that had fallen, suddenly changed and blew straight from us to the sheep. Up went all their heads in an instant, and, though we were a good eight hundred yards away, my heart stopped beating as I thought that it was all up! but, after a pause that seemed an age, during which they stood like statues, they moved slowly and suspiciously away and disappeared over a pink-coloured ridge. We got up, and ran hastily in a stooping position (no easy matter when you are at

16,000 feet), until we reached this ridge at a point some way above the place where the nyan had crossed it, and then started cautiously down the spur. At last we saw them, lying down some two hundred yards below us, and, though there was no chance of our getting a yard nearer to them this way, sorely tempted as I was, I refused the risk of shooting at this distance, accordingly we had to retreat backwards flat on our faces up the ridge until we got out of sight. Then, hastily descending the right-hand slope of the ridge, we began to creep directly towards them. At length I raised my head, and there they were. I could only see three of them; one, the biggest, was lying looking straight towards us, whilst the two others were gazing into the valley below. I had made up my mind to keep to the maxim of all good shikaris, and never to fire at an animal when lying down; but seeing a good nyan ram with his white waistcoat offering a splendid mark at about one hundred and twenty yards, I threw caution to the winds. The difficulty was that, owing to the roughness of the intervening ground, I could not bring the sights to bear on him as I lay there prone on my face, so, with a calmness of desperation, I slowly assumed a kneeling position and fired. Whether they were so surprised to see a human being rise out of the ground close to them when they had no thought of any being within fifty miles, or what it was, I cannot say; but the fact remains that they all stopped lying there for some seconds, while I took aim. I thought that I heard the bullet tell; but in a second they were up and over the brow of the spur below them, and I fired my second barrel at another as he disappeared, much as if I had been shooting at a snipe with a gun.

Springing up, I looked, and saw all four of them careering away up the nalah untouched. My feelings can be better imagined than described. I had had a better chance at nẏan than falls to the lot of most men who have spent their lives in the pursuit of Himalayan game, and had made a mess of it. Salia at once set out on the tracks of the herd. He persisted that both nẏan had been hit, while Saibra said that he had seen the first one stagger before he was on his feet; but I had watched them going away at a gallop, and said to myself they were either clean missed or only grazed. However, it was not without a gleam of hope that I ran down the slope to look at the track where they had gone along the valley, and I half expected to see blood. Not a drop! and I felt inclined to anathematise an unkind fate rather than my own bad shooting (which, by-the-by, I find is the usual impulse on like occasions). Wearily I climbed up to Saibra, who had remained on the spot from whence I had fired the shot, and never did slope seem so steep or breathing so difficult. But what is this? He has a smiling face, and tells me that as he watched the disappearing

A SUMMER IN HIGH ASIA.

flock through the glasses one ram turned away from it and made his faltering way up-hill. At the same moment a wolf, whom we could see sitting on his haunches about half a mile above us, set up a prolonged howl. Could he have smelt blood? It was a joyous sound, and I don't think that I would have fired at that wolf even if he had come within shot (which, by the way, is a pretty safe thing to say, as he wouldn't have done it). Soon afterwards Salia returned, having followed the remaining three nyan, and said that there was blood upon their tracks too. Welcome news—then both were hit! After climbing down and verifying this latter fact, I lunched by the stream, and never did cold goose taste so good! The first ram had turned away from the flock and gone for about a mile up a hill, where he had lain down and died; he was shot through the chest, the bullet passing close to the heart. The second, which was not retrieved till the following day, was hit rather far back, and had gone seven or eight miles. These facts showed me two things, firstly, the extraordinary vitality of these sheep, and secondly, that a ·450 Express bullet is not heavy enough to drop them dead, unless the bullet divides the spinal cord or tells in some absolutely vital spot. The head of the first ram, though much broken at the tips, as is the case with nearly all old rams, measured forty-two and a half inches, and was as heavy a load as two men, relieving one another, could carry back to camp;

the horns of the second were thirty-seven and a half inches in length, but in girth at the base beat those of the larger one, being eighteen inches in circumference as compared with seventeen and a half. The two were a satisfactory right and left! I now felt happy, having got two good specimens of nẙan, and resolved to quit the ground on the morrow and hand it over to H., though I dare say that with Chering Doorji's assistance I could have had a shot at some more big ones had I wished to do so. On my way back to camp I saw a kyang on some ground where it was easy to stalk him. I had no desire to shoot the beast, but my Tartar retinue were clamoring for the flesh, and what decided me, being of much more importance, was the fact that my servants' chaplis and the leather coverings of the kiltas were quite worn out, and the hide would do admirably to repair them. So the poor beast had to suffer.

I stalked to within a hundred yards of him, and hoped to drop him in his tracks, but he caught sight of me, and bounded forward just as I pressed the trigger, with the result that he was hit far back. He went on for some way and lay down, and I felt quite ill, and as if I had murdered a horse; so I sent Salia to finish him. However, the chaplis and kiltas were repaired, and the camp feasted, so one has no right to be sentimental. I was subsequently told that I should have eaten some of the flesh, as it is equal to good beef; also that British "sports-

A SUMMER IN HIGH ASIA.

men" have been known to hunt and slay kyang, and have had their heads set up as trophies of the chase! Having got these nẏan I felt more than repaid for the hundreds of miles that I had marched, and sent off a messenger to H. to tell him that *I* had shot my forty inches, and was leaving for England.

As I started on the following morning I received a note from H., with the news that he had shot a forty-two incher in Koyul and was jubilant, so that I only beat him by the odd half inch. I had got my nẏan, it is true, but had still to own myself defeated by the goa, so I returned to Hanlé, determined to spare neither time nor trouble to secure this pretty little gazelle. I may here say that I subsequently discovered that the animals that Ullia had seen on the eventful morning when I bagged my nẏan, and had hesitated whether to obey his summons or that of Saibra, were nāpoo, of which during the day he saw flocks of thirty, twenty, and seventeen, so that a sportsman camping in the spot where I was would, with any luck, probably get some of these sheep.

CHAPTER IX.

I HAD been told and had also read, that *the* place *par excellence* for goa was on the undulating ranges that rise to the south-west of the Hanlé plain, accordingly it was towards this ground that I bent my steps. We climbed a long but easy ascent to the top of the first stony ridge, on the far side of which is a big bare plateau, that looks as if made for goa, but here we saw nothing; up yet one more ridge, where we began to find respiration difficult; at the top of this another plateau (the country hereabouts consists of a series of barren "steppes"). On this plain we made out large herds of kyang, and it was said to be a favourite resort of gazelle, but we did not see any till afternoon, when we made out a herd of does, accompanied by a single buck. My bad luck after the goa (unlike my singularly good fortune after other animals) stuck to me this day, and finding it impossible to get near the buck, who, of course, always kept on the side of the herd that was farthest from me, I at length fired some long shots at him, needless to say without effect, as he looked very, very small and kept hopping about so. Next day, however, I had my revenge. After a bitterly cold night and hard frost (August 25th), I set out for the plateau above the camp where we had seen the goa on the previous afternoon. Saibra and Chering Doorji, who had gone on early, reported having seen nothing but does. Not long afterwards, however, as we were peering over the edge of the plateau, Ullia, who was with me, descried five specks some way below us, and on looking through the telescope we found that they were bucks, but the wary little beasts had caught sight of a head peering over the crest and had moved off. They did not go far, however, but began to feed. It was best to give them a little time to recover from their surprise, so I sat down and smoked a pipe for about half-an-hour. I am quite sure that one of the great secrets of this sort of shooting is not to hurry your stalk, but to give the animal lots of time, though one's natural impulse, more especially after one has been marching for, it may be, some weeks, and has at last got the long wished-for game in sight, is to go straight for him and slay him. I suppose that this arises from a sort of feeling that, unless it is done at once, he will move off and be no more seen; but if this feeling can be overcome, I am sure that it pays in the long run, even if one has to wait till the next day, or even longer, before one gets a favourable shot. As Ward says, "Many of us will march for a month to get on to Ovis Ammon ground, and yet will not consent to wait a few days after the game is sighted," and the same rule holds good for all shooting in Thibet. On this occasion, however, after the lapse of half-an-hour the goa all lay down, gazing into the valley below, and heedless of danger from above. After going for some little way along the ridge we began the descent. It was by no means bad climbing, but the danger consisted in making a noise by dislodging loose shale, which would at once have put the game on the alert.

I have noticed that in Baltistan stones dislodged, or even a shot fired, will often only cause an animal to look up in surprise, so accustomed is he in these parts to falling rocks and thunder-claps; but in Ladakh it is very different, and a slip on the shaly hill-side will usually send the game away, probably off the ground altogether, at any rate for that day. In this case my shikaris (or rather shikari, as I only took Saibra with me, telling the others to wait above), with his bare feet, and myself with felt-soled Chaplis, moved very quietly, and, when we judged that we must be about on a level with the gazelle we crept on our faces towards them. The wind, for a wonder, was steady; and at last we saw a pair of horns above an intervening ridge, and not more than eighty yards distant. I got into a kneeling position, and the goa all jumped to their feet and stood for a second, which second proved fatal to one of them, as he dropped in his tracks, shot through the heart. I am afraid that I fired more than one shot at the others as they bolted, but without success; however, the spell was at last broken, and there lay the goa with a nice head of about twelve inches. I really think that, as I contemplated him, I felt almost more satisfaction than I had done after any of the previous shots that I had made. When his head had been despatched to camp we followed the remaining four bucks, as these animals do not, as a rule, go far before stopping again; but though we saw them soon afterwards about a mile away, and stalked up to within fifty yards of them, they heard us approaching, and bolted before I could get a shot, owing to a hillock that was between me and them. From the spot where we now were the view was one of the wildest that I had seen even in this wild country. To the south the high mountains towards Chumurti and the frontier of Chinese Thibet are less than a day's march distant, and seem to be of a more rugged and snowy character than any that I had lately seen. To the east runs the steep ridge that separates the Hanlé Valley from that of Koyul, while to the north the Lanak range and the road to the Tso-Moriri close the view.

Far below us was the green patch that represented the Hanlé plain, with the monastery looking like a white speck, the latter being the only sign of the existence of human beings in this wilderness of barren mountains. As we were making our way back towards camp, we observed a herd of doe gazelle on the hill above us, and hoping that there might be some bucks with them, we began the stalk. We had not gone far, and were just topping a ridge, when a nice buck, coming from the opposite direction, met us face to face at about seventy yards. I fired at him point-blank, and to my surprise (as a goa end on is not a large mark for a standing shot) hit him hard. Off he went downhill with the does, but presently separated from them and went and lay down in the middle of the plain at the bottom of the hill. Cautiously descending, we crept towards him, crawling flat on our faces across the sharp stones, and dropping every time that he lifted his head. After about half-a-mile of this pleasant work I got another shot, and as he did not rise, thought that I had finished him; but just as Ullia was about to seize him by the horns, having run forward to "hallal" him, he got up and went off again; but not far this time, and another bullet gave him his quietus. He carried a nice head with horns of twelve and a half inches, and thicker than those of the one that I had killed in the morning. I reached camp that afternoon in a contented frame of mind, having now obtained good specimen heads of every animal that I might expect to meet in these regions, excepting the shāpoo, whose acquaintance I hoped to make during my homeward journey. On reaching camp I found a jubilant note from H., who had

HIMIS MONASTERY.

killed a big nyan, and was now encamped only some twelve miles away in search of goa.

The following day (August 26th) I set out on my homeward journey, and that evening pitched my tent at an encamping-ground called Poongook, picturesquely situated on the banks of the Hanlé river.

During the afternoon I went up the stream and shot some teal and a duck, and saw some female nāpoo on the heights above. Our route now lay across a plain to the Lanak-La, as I had determined to make my way back to Leh by the Tso Moriri, that beautiful salt lake whose scenery has never failed to impress anyone who has seen it. We camped at the foot of the pass, where a long valley runs in from the northward, passing through a country which looks as if it would well repay a visit from the sportsman in search of nyan or nāpoo. Here, in the stream, my servants caught (much to the detriment of the butterfly-net in which they were captured) some delicious little fish like trout, which, when cooked by Sekour Khan, were an unwonted luxury.

On the morning of August 28th, having sent on all the yāks, I started about 7.30 to cross the Lanak-La. The gradient of this pass is easy, but from the difficulty of respiration, and the fact that the peaks of Sidomba (20,405 feet), and an unnamed one (21,038 feet), did not appear to be much above us on either hand, it must be a fairly high one: I should think probably some 17,000 or 18,000 feet. On the summit I saw some specimens of the *Vanessa Ladakensis* butterfly, and in the foolishness of my heart thought to capture them; but, after running twenty yards, found that I was as beat as if I had run a mile at a lower elevation, added to which the sun-glare off the stones was such that one lost sight of them completely when they were only a few yards away. The view from the summit of this pass westwards is magnificent, over the lower red and yellow hills that surround the Tso Moriri to the barrier of snows that divides Ladakh from Spiti and Zanskar.

Going on some way farther, we pitched our camp at Dongan, near the marshy border of a stream, and here I put up two snipe, but, of course, had not my gun with me at the time. When I did get it, and went to look if there were any more, equally of course, I saw none. The following day we struck northwards over some low hills, said to be a favourite resort of goa. We had not gone far before we saw two nice bucks, which, however, had been alarmed, probably by our yāks, which were going along at the foot of the hill, and which went and lay down near some kyang. Oh, those kyang! Three times did we stalk the goa, and on each occasion, just as I flattered myself that we were nearly within shot, the brutes of kyang began to snort and dance about, effectually putting the goa on the alert, and taking them off for about a mile up hill every time. This sort of thing was getting monotonous, and the work arduous, when at last the kyang went off in one direction whilst the goa took the opposite one.

After a long stalk I got to within a hundred and fifty yards of the latter, who were far below us and lying down, and, waiting till one got up, I fired and dropped him; I now turned my attention to the second one, but never got a fair chance at him as he galloped away. Looking at the first one I saw that he had risen, and was going slowly away, hit through the shoulder, as we could see by the glasses from the blood. Very foolishly (I really ought to have known better by this time) I followed him up at once, with the natural result that he gradually quickened his pace, and though he was pursued for many hours, we never got him. The fact was, that seeing him bleeding copiously from the shoulder, I thought that he would not be able to go far, but the wound must have been a merely superficial one, and, as I had fired from almost immediately above him, had probably only grazed the shoulder. In the middle of the day we halted not far from one of the salt lakes typical of these regions, the waters of which were of a brilliant blue colour. This lake is surrounded by yellow and red hills (one very curious one, almost overhanging the lake, looks as if it has a ruined castle on top of it), the name is Lam Tso. Farther away are forbidding precipices and the lofty snow-clad summits that are crossed by the Parang-La (18,600 feet), which is on the road

A SUMMER IN HIGH ASIA.

from Simla to Leh. Whenever we halted in these bleak regions, if it was afternoon and the daily gale had begun to blow, I improvised the following shelter, which may be found of use to visitors in these parts, as very often one cannot find even a convenient boulder behind which to crouch on the barren wastes. Opening an umbrella I placed it on the ground, head to wind, and, as it would of course have been blown away immediately if left to itself, I used to cover it with a blanket well weighted down all round with stones or gravel. This formed a fair shelter alike from scorching sun and freezing wind, to both of which one is exposed simultaneously in this pleasant climate, and made a fairly comfortable resting-place until it was time to continue the march, or till the tents arrived, on occasions when I happened to be the first to arrive at our camping-ground. We saw several more gazelle that day, but I did not go after them, and we finally reached the end of our march, a place called Ooti, rather late in the evening. Here our camp was pitched on what might (by a slight stretch of imagination) be likened to a bit of Scotch moor, the ground being boggy and tussocky.

The next morning, just as I was going to breakfast before starting, I saw a sand-grouse come down to drink, and shot him; and knowing the habits of the bird from frequent encounters with him in Egypt and India, I sent on all the camp, but waited behind myself, thinking that probably flocks

"THIS LAKE IS SURROUNDED BY YELLOW AND RED HILLS."

of them would come down later for a like purpose. Nor was I disappointed, as at about 9 A.M. they began arriving in parties. I shot three and a half brace for food and skins, and then continued on my way. A little farther on we came across a hen sand-grouse with two chicks, from whom she tried to lure us by the method so often adopted by birds, of running on herself apparently wounded and unable to fly. Of course we left the young ones in peace. My pleasure at having bagged the sand-grouse (the only ones, by the way, that I noticed during the whole trip) was somewhat damped when I met Saibra near this spot, and he told me that he had seen a magnificent lynx, and had followed it for some way, hoping that it might lie down and await my arrival : but it was disobliging and had declined to do so. I should much have liked to have seen, and possibly to have got a shot at, so rare a beast. We soon climbed up this Pass, which presented the features usual in a Ladakhi road ; but there were two familiar denizens of these wastes that I noticed in greater numbers in this particular place than I had done anywhere else. The first of these were the lizards, that swarm everywhere in the stones, and which, owing to their colour and the glare, and the rapidity with which they move, are often almost invisible. The second were the locusts or crickets, of a sort which seems peculiar to Rupshu, and which are to be met with in great numbers in some places. They again are of the same colour as the stones, and you do not notice them until they rise with a loud clicking whirr, which continues while they pursue a short flight, during which their wings, of a dark blue colour with a band of a lighter shade across them, are very visible, and which only ceases as they fall and are again lost to sight amongst the stones.

From the summit of this Pass I got my first glimpse of the famous Tso-Moriri. This lake is at an altitude of about 15,000 feet, and there being no visible outlet for its waters, must be kept to its level by evaporation; Macintyre says that it is "almost, if not quite, the highest of known lakes in the world." It is some fifteen miles long and four or five wide,

SUNSET ON THE TSO-MORIRI.

and is famed for the grandeur of its scenery. It would be an impossibility to describe its beauty (enhanced as it was on the day on which I travelled along its banks, by the brilliancy of the weather); indeed, as Drew says of another of the Ladakhi lakes, "It is difficult to persuade one's self that it is not as beautiful as can be." The water itself is of a most lovely translucent blue, which admits of your seeing the bottom quite clearly, and which seems to be a peculiarity of these salt lakes, and when broken into ripples by the wind, the light shines through the waves and makes them look of the colour of a sapphire. The sandy shores are in places covered with a coarse, thin-growing grass of a vivid green, and are surrounded with richly-coloured sandstone hills, while on the western side magnificent crags rise up to the higher snows. Beneath these crags is perched the little village of Karzok, said to be the highest in the world, at an altitude of 14,960 feet above the sea-level. It consists of a gonpa or monastery, standing on a hillock, with a few huts clustered round the foot. Though called a salt lake, the water has only a slightly brackish taste, but the natives, and even the yāks, refuse to drink it. As we had foolishly brought no fresh water with us, we had a long, hot, and thirsty double march along the eastern shore, passing the famous Nÿan Nalahs, Shāpgo and Luglang, in the dry watercourses of which I saw some good horns, and were not sorry to arrive at our camping-ground, Peldo Le, at the head of the lake, late in the evening. I had been about ten hours in the saddle, and the men on foot must have had about enough of it. On this day Baboo Lal and Sekour Khan had walked, as I had been obliged to give their pony to Ramzahn, who started early and went round to Karzok to get flour for the camp, as we had run out of this commodity.

Whilst we were pitching camp I saw some bar-headed geese—stalked, and shot one. Here one of the yāks, being rather hot and tired, rolled in the water before being unloaded. Nice yāk! Of course he was the one who was carrying the tent and some spare clothes! The following morning our way still led to the northwards over the high plateau separating us from the Polakonka Pass. At first we went up a pretty valley with lots of grass, where we came across a Chang-Pa encampment, and then climbed up to the high table-land. A little adventure that befel me by the way was that whilst trying to hold my pony, which was bolting, the native-made bit broke, and in this powerless condition I charged right into the middle of the Tartar camp, much to the astonishment of the inhabitants thereof; our wild career being eventually checked by a tent-rope, which brought pony, rider, and tent down in a confused heap, none of them, luckily, the worse for the adventure. When we arrived on the plateau a wonderful view lay before us. To the east, and far below us, was the small bright blue lake, Tso-Kiagr, and the road by Nakpagoding to Puga, while to the west was a range of hills that look made for nāpoo and nẙan.

That evening we camped on the high ground at 18,000 feet, or more (probably more), our highest camp, and when morning broke we found the whole country covered with hard-frozen snow. That morning we climbed down hill for some distance, and eventually reached the summit of the Polakonka Pass above Puga. As this spot is about 16,300 feet high, and we had been descending

THE CHAGZOT AND LAMAS OF THE HIMIS MONASTERY.

steadily for four hours, our camp of the previous night must have been pretty high. Whilst resting here I observed a peculiar phenomenon. It was about midday, there was a heavy storm over the peaks to the eastwards, and the sun was shining vaguely from a misty sky, while all round, and at some distance from it, was a halo as bright in its prismatic colours as a rainbow. I fancy that it may have been caused by ice-particles in the atmosphere, but have never observed it before or since. That evening we arrived at our old camping-place, Thugji, but not till after we had made a very long and disagreeable march. The wind blew with more than ordinary fury, and the last few miles through heavy sand, after a long day's work, were very trying. Night fell as we reached the camping-place, and the tents being, of course, on the last yāks, it was pitch dark long before they were put up.

The following day we rested in camp, and I took a gun and went round the Salt Lake, getting a few geese and "Brahminy" ducks, also a specimen of the Thibetan fox (*Vulpes Ferrilatus*), a pretty little animal with lovely fur. On this occasion I noticed and examined the very curious horizontal lines, "ice-margin" marks, as Drew calls them, that run round the basin of the Tso-Kar, and which would tend to show that the lake, or more correctly, lakes (as there are two, one salt and one fresh), are gradually drying up.

A SUMMER IN HIGH ASIA.

On the following morning we moved round the end of the lake by Puttatuktuk (home of the goa), and encamped at a place that rejoices in the name of Pongonogo, and the next day (September 3rd) struck the main Simla-Leh road, and journeyed on to Debring, at the foot of the Tagalang Pass. On reaching this well-known track I felt that I was fairly back in civilisation, and we camped half-way up the Pass, at about 17,000 feet, where it snowed all night, and was bitterly cold. On the way to Debring we had a glimpse along the Zara Valley towards Zanskar, and this nalah was apparently closed by some terrific-looking mountains of the organ-pipe type, which appeared as bad as those that I had seen in the Hushe Nalah. In the morning we climbed the short ascent that remained at the top of the Tagalang Pass (17,500 feet) and descended on the opposite side by a rocky ravine. Here I shot with my small rifle a splendid lammergeier, or bearded vulture, which was drinking at a stream, and which measured nine feet from tip to tip of the wings.*

Soon afterwards we reached the village of Gya, where I had encamped some six weeks previously. As I looked back to that time I thought of how much I had done during those six weeks, and of what extraordinarily good luck I had experienced. Then I had not had a shot at Thibetan game, and at the most hoped to get a few nāpoo, and perhaps

* Now in the Norwich Museum.

A SUMMER IN HIGH ASIA.

a small nyăn, now I was returning with good nāpoo and goa, and had got three nyăn, including one head which alone would have been worth the trouble of many expeditions. Apart from sport, I had experienced a most delightful time; the weather had been favourable, the natives disposed to show me sport (owing to the kindness of the Wazir and the Chagzōt), and none of my party had fallen ill or met with an accident.

I had made the acquaintance of a singular and most interesting country, and though the description of the absolute barrenness of the sun-scorched, wind-swept plains of these altitudes, with their absence of vegetation and their salt-lakes, sounds unattractive enough, yet such is not really the case. There is an extraordinary fascination to the traveller about these vast, silent solitudes, with their many-coloured hills and bright blue lakes, which even the discomfort of scorching sun and ever-present wind (which latter, indeed, is acknowledged by all who have been in these parts to be the greatest drawback), and the minor inconveniences of difficulty in respiration and the occasional absence of fresh water and fuel, fail wholly to dissipate, and I am sure that most men who have travelled in these highlands will look back with pleasure to their memories, to the feeling of freedom and unrestraint with which they roamed over the rolling hills and lofty valleys of Rupshu.*

* For butterflies of Rupshu, see Appendix

CHAPTER X.

OF the animals at which I might hope to get a shot, the shāpoo alone now remained, curious that the first animal that I had seen (in Hushe) was to be the last I was to shoot. I had passed by much ground well known to be good for shāpoo on my march up the Indus (to whose valley and that of the Shyok this species of sheep seems to be more or less confined), but had left it untouched, being on other game intent. Now I was determined to get a good head, though I expected that having left it till the last, I should find this task, as is so often the case, the hardest. H., who had secured a very fine pair of horns before going up to Rupshu, had recommended two good grounds, one on the opposite side of the Indus from Upshi, and the other, the side ravine that joins the main Miru Nalah at the village of that name. As the latter would be on my way, I determined to try it first. We set out from Gya (where I had lost myself in ecstatic contemplation of a tree, the first that I had seen for many a week) on September 5th, and soon turned down into the Miru gorge. This ravine, to my mind, had lost nothing of its extraordinary character for rugged outline and bizarre colouring, and, though I had seen much of this sort of ground since my previous experience of the valley, I was still of opinion that it was the finest and most striking view of the kind that I had come across. On reaching the village of Miru we turned eastwards up the valley that runs down from the range on the west side of the Tubbuh branch of the Gya Nalah; and here I particularly noticed the curious conglomerate rock of which the cliffs are largely composed, and which sometimes consists of most brilliantly coloured stones and pebbles which are imbedded in the solidified mud. Moorcraft describes it as "a sort of pudding stone."

The air was now quite soft and warm, very different to the icy blasts of the higher regions (we had descended to 13,000 feet). This side ravine is a very barren one, and at first very narrow, being shut in on either side by exceedingly steep hills of shale, but about three miles higher up it becomes wider, rocky precipices showing themselves behind these slopes. At this point I encamped, and the very same evening we discovered, through the glasses, a flock of seven shāpoo rams, high up on the hills above the camp; but it was too late to pursue them then.

The next day I was off after them at an early hour, and during the morning had some really bad climbing along the face of shale slopes some

A SUMMER IN HIGH ASIA.

hundreds of feet above the valley, whose stones went rolling down at every step till they fell into the abysses below. Here, for the first time, I found that English shooting-boots were better to wear than the ordinary Pula or grass-shoe, or even Chaplis. About 10 A.M. we viewed the shāpoo on the opposite side of a deep valley, which it would have taken me hours to circumvent, during which time they would probably have moved away, so that there was nothing for it but to lie down and wait. During this period of waiting I had an excellent opportunity of watching these sheep through the glasses; some lay down and slept, some grazed, some played about, but one always acted as a sentinel and kept watch, being in his turn relieved by another. On one occasion two rams had a butting match, and the shock of their meeting was plainly audible across the valley some seconds after the impact, though I must have been fully a mile distant at the time.

About 4 o'clock in the afternoon the flock moved off towards the head of the valley, and, hoping that they would cross it and come along our side, Salia set off to meet them. Never shall I forget that scramble! We had certainly kept the best (or worst) till the last. I was dragged along a slope of shale so steep that if we stopped for a moment to take breath, not only ourselves, but the whole hillside, commenced sliding down towards the precipices in which the slope terminated far below; occasionally Ramzahn, who was with us, had to stick his Khud stick into the hillside to give me something to step upon for a foothold; but we were to be rewarded, and eventually saw the shāpoo coming towards us, and also that they were all good rams. A little farther on and we suddenly saw them seventy yards above us, and at the same moment they saw us, and began scrambling up the hill. Fortunately this was so steep that even they couldn't go very fast; but what a position for a shot! I could hardly keep my feet, was panting for breath, and could of course neither kneel nor lie down on such a slope. Without a moment's hesitation Salia seized me in his arms to steady me, and I fired as best I might. The recoil of the second shot sent Salia, self, and rifle flying down the hillside, and when we pulled up we were just in time to see the shāpoo going over the crest. I counted them, one, two, three, four, five, six—a pause—we did not see a seventh go over, but he might have crossed by a gully out of sight. Salia and I could not tell whether the shots had told, but Ramzahn said that nothing was hit; so we wended our way down to the stream at the bottom of the ravine and quenched our thirst.

I must say that I was hardly surprised at having missed them, taking into consideration the circumstances of the shot. While we were resting here, Saibra, who had the telescope, and who had been on the opposite side of the valley, came bounding down the rocks like an ibex, and said, "We shall get him all right!" "Get whom?" said I, not in the best of tempers. "Why, the shāpoo, of course," answered Saibra. "I shouted to you that he was hit when he turned away from the flock; didn't you hear me?"

Now, considering that Saibra was at least half-a-mile away at the time, and that Salia and I were busy rolling down a hill, it was scarcely strange that I had not done so; nevertheless, it was joyful news. I have to confess to having been too done to go after him, so sent Ullia and Ramzahn, and they brought in his head, a nice one of twenty-seven and a half inches—nothing out of the way, but quite good enough. Whilst on our way back to camp we saw a large flock of ewes and small rams, about forty in number, who came down to the main stream to drink, so that there were evidently lots of shāpoo in the nalah, and also, I should say, judging from the horns lying about, many nāpoo. On the following day we reached Upshi, and were once more on the banks of the Indus. A curious thing happened here whilst I was in my tent, lying on my bed reading. It was about 3 P.M. when I suddenly heard a rushing noise and a crash, and found myself still lying on my bed, but in the open field. A whirlwind, or shaitan (devil), as it is called by the natives, had come past, and had taken my tent clean away. My things were blown in every direction, an iron basin having been carried twenty yards

CHURTENS AND MANI ON THE ROAD BELOW HIMIS.

(measured). There was no damage done, save that a little brandy was spilled out of a bottle hanging on the tent-pole. Babu Lal declared that the "shaitan" had come in, had a drink, and continued on his way rejoicing. A lot of my clothes, which had been washed and were drying in the sun, were whirled up almost out of sight, but were eventually retrieved.

The next day I arrived at Machalang, and here I was joined by H., who, having shot his nÿan and goa, had made double marches to catch me up. We went on next day to the famous Monastery of Himis. This "Gonpa" has been described so often and so well that I will only attempt to write my own impressions of this most curious place. H. had paid it a previous visit, having been here on his way up to Rupshu, and his visit was made during the "fair time." This, of course, is the best time to see it, as then Lamaists in hundreds, many of them from a considerable distance, congregate here, and a regular festival is held, part of the performance consisting of those curious religious plays or dances, with their grotesque masks, which are so important a feature of the Buddhist religion.

On my way up the Indus I had passed the entrance to the Himis Nalah without noticing it—in fact, there is nothing in the view from the main valley to show that this rocky ravine is different from any other of the many side nalahs in these deserts. About a mile up this ravine, however,

A SUMMER IN HIGH ASIA.

you turn a corner and come on a strange and unlooked-for spectacle. In a small amphitheatre, surrounded by very precipitous rocks that run up to the snows, is a patch of cultivation and a considerable grove of trees. Above these, and built on, or rather into, the side of the hill, is the Monastery, a large, rambling building with many courtyards and balconied windows, a line round the top being, as usual, painted red, and the roof itself ornamented with yāks' tails on poles, strings of coloured flags, and also, here, with some umbrella-like erections, whether for ornament or use I was unable to discover. Clustered outside the walls of the Gonpa is a small village, and the surrounding points of rock are crowned with Churtens and tombs. When we arrived, the Lamas were at work in the fields, singing the quaint Ladakhi song.

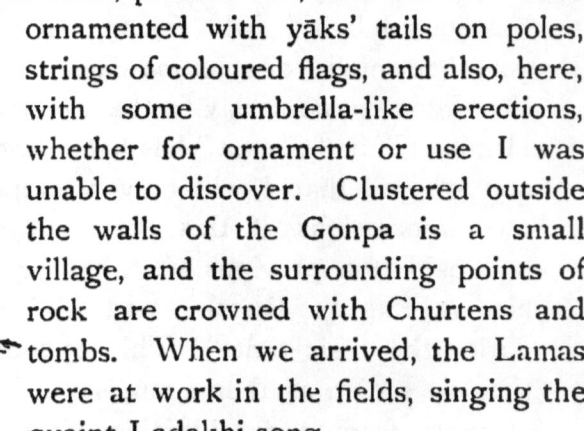

YOUNG BUDDHIST RED LAMA.

We pitched our camp in the midst of the grove, and after luncheon proceeded to view the monastery. We first ascended through a garden with many flowers, chiefly asters, poppies, marigolds, &c., in bloom, and passing by some quaint old paintings on the walls, entered a courtyard. Here we were greeted by the ferocious-looking dogs that are always chained up in a Thibetan monastery. We were conducted by an unusually dirty Lama in clothes of a dull red colour, and with a shaven head, and, of course, the right arm bare, through the courtyards, with high masts, paintings on the walls, and innumerable cylindrical prayer-wheels, which were let into the walls in horizontal rows, so that a hand run along them (much as a boy will run a stick along area-railings in London) sets them all in motion and brings the devout Buddhist nearer to Nirvana.

We entered some of the temples which were filled with silk banners, and innumerable figures of the Buddha and other deities, some of the latter being of large size and profusely ornamented, much gilding and even precious stones being employed. Before many of these figures, offerings of food, flowers, and lighted lamps were placed, and some of the shrines were decorated with vases of valuable metals and porcelain, which, I conclude, came from China. We also saw the library, with its shelves covered with books, each one of which consists of roughly printed strips of parchment or paper enclosed between two flat boards.

Here also were many weird musical instruments, consisting, for the most part, of different kinds of trumpets and drums upon which the Lamas, I should say from experience, practise at odd hours during the day and night. It is a curious and rather impressive place, and, though there is nothing grand about it, yet there is a sort of quaint air of mystery which is very fascinating, and which is usually to be found in a Buddhist monastery, though perhaps the rock-temples of Buddha in Ceylon are more impressive and weird than these Gonpas of the red Lama. Of course the neighbourhood of this sacred spot is more extensively ornamented than ever with religious symbols, and there are Churtens without number, and piles of "mani" stones of great length.

The following day we started for Leh, making a short halt at Golab-Bagh to change the beasts of burden, and riding along the green pastures by the Indus and through the village of Chushot (which, by the way, was not all joy, as the inhabitants had turned the path into a watercourse by running off all the irrigation channels into it, thereby undermining and bringing down the loose stone walls on either side, so that we were soon splashed with mud from head to foot). We arrived soon after midday at Leh, and here, thanks to the Commissioner's kindness, though he himself was away, I put up at the Residency, and slept under a civilized roof, and was fed on civilized food, for the first time after many weeks of roughing it.

The Residency of our Joint-Commissioner at Leh stands in a large enclosure, where there are some really good trees, channels of running water and green turf, as well as some bright flowers in front of the house, and appears a veritable oasis after travelling in the stony deserts of Ladakh for many weary marches. H. and I remained for a few days at Leh, which at this time of year is a very busy place, the bazaar being crowded with people of many nationalities.

The Central Asians from Yarkand, with their quilted robes, little fur caps and long boots, are accommodated with their many horses in a large

A SUMMER IN HIGH ASIA.

and well-kept caravanserai, which is well worth a visit from anyone who is in search of the picturesque; whilst in the main street of the town are to be seen merchants from Thibet, mysterious Lhassa, and even China, mixing with the Kashmiris and Indians from the cities of the plain. Of course there are many Ladakhis and also some Baltis, Chang-Pa, and wild-looking men from Rudok, whilst the ever-present Indian "bunnia"* plies his trade on either side of the street. It is a brilliant and striking scene this mart, where the goods of Central Asia are exchanged for those of India; and to anyone who sees it, suggests the question of the possibilities of the trade between Central Asia and India. This struck me particularly, and, as a result of inquiries that I made, and the kindness of Captain Godfrey in giving me information and statistics, I formed the opinion which, with my reasons for doing so, I shall endeavour to explain in another chapter.

* Shopkeeper.

BUDDHIST SILVER AND COPPER SHRINE BOX, AND METAL OPIUM PIPE.

"H." AND THE AUTHOR, WITH THEIR LADAKH TROPHIES.

CHAPTER XI.

ON the 15th of September H. and I bid farewell to Captain Godfrey, who had returned, and started on our journey back to Kashmir. The first day we traversed the barren road that leads to Snemo, which I have already described when on my way up to Leh, and on our arrival found the camp pitched and a meal prepared, as we had sent everything on ahead the previous day. The next march took us to Saspul, past picturesque Bazgo. As we crossed the high plateau we got a magnificent view, across the river, of the crags on either side of the Zanskar stream, which here flows into the Indus; they looked very grand, but very inacces-

A SUMMER IN HIGH ASIA.

sible. In the orchard where we encamped at Saspul were many apple-trees covered with rosy fruit, but the apricots were all over. The next day's march brought us to Snurla, and we had not been there long before Captain Godfrey arrived, being on his way down to Srinagar with all possible speed. He had started from Leh that morning, and had done fifty-six miles by about 2 P.M., pretty good going along a mountain road. He was in a hurry to get down to see the Resident of Kashmir, who was leaving, and accomplished the journey (two hundred and fifty miles) in under four days. Of course, he had relays of good ponies; but still, when it is remembered that the road (though in fair order at this time) crosses the main range of the Himalaya, the performance must certainly be regarded as a good one. The distance is nineteen ordinary marches. With Captain Godfrey was old Munshi Palgez, who was accompanying him as far as the frontier of Ladakh, that is, to Kargil. On the 18th we started for Lamayuru. As far as Khalsi the road was known to me, but at the latter place we left the path which had brought me up, on the right bank of the river, from the Chorbat Pass and Baltistan, and crossed by the bridge (the scene of the famous exploit, before-mentioned, of the two officers who were racing for a nalah) to the left bank. At Khalsi, where we stopped for a short time to rest the horses, a small ibex and shāpoo head were brought to us in the hope that

A SUMMER IN HIGH ASIA.

we might buy them, and, of course, we indignantly refused.

It is, very rightly, against the game laws of Kashmir for any native to offer a head for sale, and we threatened to report the man for doing so; but the very fact of his showing them to us looks as if he knew that occasionally a "Sahib" would not be averse to (shall we say it?) *add* to his bag in this way. A few miles below Khalsi we left the Indus Valley for good, and turned southwards up the fine gorge where the streams from Lamayuru and Wanla come down, having united some little way farther up it. This ravine is a magnificent sight, being very narrow, with the rushing torrent hemmed in on either side by tremendous precipices. I was told that it is quite equal to the Khyber, Bholan, and other more celebrated passes. After crossing the stream at a point where the Wanla torrent comes down from the eastwards (I have been told that this latter direction is *the* one for anyone to take who is in search of nāpoo), we ascended the bed of the stream, sometimes wading in the water itself, which was fortunately not deep. Here one of H.'s ponies (luckily not the one which was carrying his horns) fell over a cliff into the stream, but, as it turned out, no serious damage was done, though the Ee, who was in his cage on top of the load, must have been considerably astonished at his sudden ducking, and was certainly not in the best of tempers on his arrival in camp.

ON THE SRINAGAI-LEH ROAD. THE MONASTERY AND VILLAGE OF LAMAYURU.

CALIFORNIA

A SUMMER IN HIGH ASIA.

Lamayuru is even more quaint than most of the Ladakhi villages. Below, in the valley, are the terraced fields, with a few habitations immediately above them, but the main part of the hamlet is perched upon the crags and pinnacles of a high cliff, which is split up into innumerable fissures, some of which are bridged across, and the houses are built on the platforms. Altogether it is a striking-looking place, many of the surrounding hills being conspicuous for the sandstone pillars, mostly surmounted by large stones, which look just like huge petrified mushrooms, and which are so often a prominent feature of these regions.

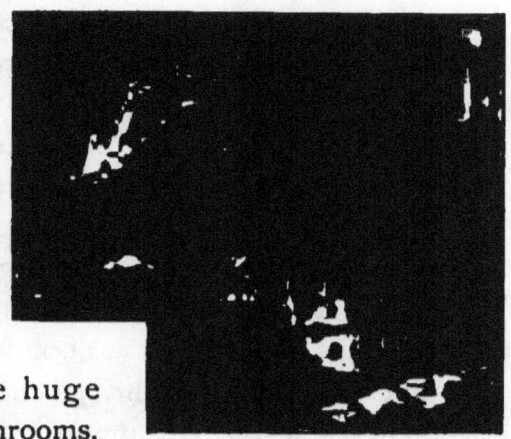

ON THE ROAD TO LEH; VILLAGE AND MONASTERY OF CHAMBA-MOULBEKH.

The road below the village is bordered by rows of innumerable Churtens and tombs of varying size. On leaving Lamayuru H. started for a day's shāpoo shooting on the Fotu-La, whilst I set out for Kharbu, the next march. The road gradually ascends up sandy, barren hills, which look (and I believe are) very good for shāpoo.

These animals, however, are here hunted by almost every sportsman who arrives from Kashmir (who, after many weary marches during which he has not had an opportunity of taking his rifle out of his case, is naturally dying to have a shot at something), and are consequently shy even beyond the habit of their kind. The summit of the Fotu Pass is 13,400 feet, and one gets a fine view of precipices to the east, and open, sandy hills to the south-west. After crossing the pass the road leads along a somewhat monotonous valley to Kharbu, where I halted. The mountains above this place on the left bank of the stream look good for ibex, and Salia told me that he had been with a "Sahib" who shot there, and had good sport. Whilst waiting for my camp to arrive, a party of strolling players coming from Leh passed me; they were in picturesque costume, and each pony was carrying two grotesque riders. The following day's march took me over another easy pass, the Namika-La (13,000 feet), in character very like the Fotu-La, and passing by the village of Wakha, and the entrance to the nalah of the same name where H. had had good sport with the ibex on his way up to Ladakh in the spring, I arrived at last at Moulbekh. I had intended to go on to Shergol, but, having been told that this stage divided the marches more evenly, and seeing a good camping-ground here, I decided to stop for the night.

 Moulbekh is a picturesque and characteristic

A SUMMER IN HIGH ASIA.

Lama village, the most noticeable feature being, as usual, a gonpa perched on the summit of a detached, and apparently inaccessible, spur of rock. Not far from the foot of this pinnacle is a colossal and much revered image of Chamba, carved out of the face of a huge monolith, which is standing in the valley near the road. At Moulbekh I found old Munshi Palgez, who had accompanied Captain Godfrey as far as the frontier of his (the Munshi's) dominions, and was now on his homeward journey. The good (but somewhat dirty) old man came to pay me a visit in my tent, and though our conversation was of necessity somewhat limited, as I could not understand very much of his rapidly spoken Punjabi, he evinced great commiseration for my wounded leg (I had been almost disabled by a bad kick from a pony a couple of days previously), and sat stroking it for a long time, assuring me that by so doing he could make it much better. The result on the following day was not quite as noticeable as he had promised me that it would be ; but the intention was kind.

The next day I passed Shergol with its rock-cut monastery, on the other side of the stream, and a feeling of sadness mingled with the pleasant anticipations of a return to civilization, as I thought that this was the last Gonpa, and almost the last heap of Mani stones that I should see, and that we were in reality leaving the quaint and mysterious region of Ladakh and its Lamas, where we had spent so pleasant a time. Riding through some narrow valleys with fine rock scenery, and passing villages which looked most fertile with the grass, willows and poplar trees, we eventually emerged, through a rocky "Derwaza," or gateway, on to the well cultivated little plain of Pushkim, where there is a considerable village. Here we camped under some poplars near the stream, and it was not long before H. arrived, having killed a shāpoo, and bringing with him W., an officer who had been shooting in the Changchenmo Valley, and had had good sport. Soon after starting from Pushkim on the following day, we arrived on a high plateau beyond which the Wakha stream joins the river that comes down the Sooroo Valley (over which Captain Godfrey and his companions had built the bridge), at whose junction is situated Kargil, the frontier village of Baltistan, and Ladakh, a place of some importance.

As we were crossing this table-land, we had fine views of the snowy peaks of Sooroo, whose side nalahs are so famous for ibex. As soon as the Sooroo River is crossed, the character of the mountains changes, and I was once more amongst my old friends (?), the steep granite ranges and precipitous ravines of Baltistan. A little farther on the road turns a corner, where the Sooroo River joins the Dras stream, and on the opposite bank of the latter I could see the path that leads down to the Indus Valley, which I had traversed on my way to Skardo. Our road lay along the narrow path cut in the face of the cliff, and occasionally crossed galleries built out from the rock, and we halted for the night at Chanagand, below which village is the bridge by which I had crossed to Kirkitchu, and so down the road to Skardo.

Already our approach to more fertile regions began to be apparent, owing to the fact that occasional rain-clouds from the storms that break on the other side of the Himalaya stray as far as this, and the barren slopes were dotted with pencil cedar, Umbu (*Mycaria*), wild currants, and rose bushes, which grew amongst the boulders and stones. At this point I joined the road which I described on my outward journey; but how different it now appeared! Independently of the fact that I was now marching daily with pleasant companions instead of by my melancholy self, I knew the road, and each day's march accordingly seemed half the distance that it did when I was "outward bound." The valleys, too, which had seemed the most desolate places imaginable after having just left the fertile Vale of Kashmir, now appeared positively luxuriant to an eye which had become accustomed to the wind-swept uplands of Rupshu and the glaring deserts of Ladakh. As we journeyed along to Tashgaum and Dras I noted each well-remembered spot that I had passed, as it now seemed, an age before.

The Plain of Dras seemed very green, and we noticed that the clouds hung heavy in the direction of the Zogi-La, promising bad weather on the top of the range; but this was of little consequence at this season of the year, as there was not much fear of fresh snow falling so early here, and the Pass itself would be a green valley instead of the snowy wilderness that we had crossed on our way up from Kashmir. The Valley of Mataiyan was as imposing as ever, and here I shot a fine specimen of the Kashmiri marmot (*Arctomys caudatus*) in his winter coat. I had some difficulty in finding one of these animals, a fact which I had not expected, considering the large numbers that I had seen in this place on my way up: I suppose that they had by this time entered their hibernating quarters. For a second time I was foiled in my attempt to cross the river opposite the camp at Mataiyan, owing to the depth of the river; but on this occasion I went about a mile lower down, and there forded the stream. The current was swift and the water up to the top of the saddle; but I got over safely, though Salia (who arrived in camp some hours later, having had to go back to Pandras, four miles lower down, to cross by the bridge) was very cross, and said that I should not have attempted it, as it was very dangerous.

These Kashmiris seem to have a wholesome dread of mountain torrents, and they are perhaps right, as the water sometimes comes down like a wall. On leaving Mataiyan the hillside became clothed with birch trees and shrubs, now glorious

RDUNGSTEN IN THE HIMIS MONASTERY.

in their autumnal tints, and the ride up to the summit of the Pass was most enjoyable. Instead of the nine miles of snow that we had experienced in May, we now beheld an expanse of grass, brilliant with wild flowers; the bitterly cold wind on the top, however, told us that it would not be long before the first snow would come and turn the Zogi-La into a wilderness of white and rock for the long winter months. On reaching the ridge that descends so precipitously into the Vale of Kashmir, the path, instead of leading straight down the nalah as it had done on our way up, when this was an ice-bound slope, led along the hillside, and then by a very steep zig-zag path down to Baltal.

Here, at the bottom of an ascent, we saw the skeletons of several ponies that had fallen and perished earlier in the season. The view from the top of the ridge into the beautiful Sindh valley, shut in by its pine-clad cliffs topped with snow, and now blazing with autumn colours, fairly took our breath away after our wanderings in stony wastes; the air, too, at once became softer and milder, and after a short delay to gaze on so fair a scene, we hastened down the path. In front of us was a long string of laden ponies going down to India from Yarkand, and as one of these ponies was turning a corner, his load caught in a projecting rock, and in a moment he was falling over and over down a slope as near perpendicular as might be, from a height some three hundred feet above the stream.

A SUMMER IN HIGH ASIA.

It made one feel sick to look at him, and I could see the poor beast lying at the bottom, moving his head slowly from side to side, as a dying animal will do. After pitching our camp I thought that I would send Ullia with my rifle to despatch the unhappy brute, as I knew that its owner, after securing the load, would leave it to die, after the manner of the Asiatic, and our astonishment may be better imagined than described when we heard that such a proceeding would be useless, not to say impolitic, as the pony, after a short rest (!) at the bottom of the ravine, had continued its journey, though somewhat cut and shaken. We could scarcely believe our ears, but it turned out to be a fact, nevertheless. This night we camped in a flowery meadow, and felt that our expedition was over.

I lingered for a fortnight in this delightful valley, camping in the pine and deodar forests, and hoping to get a shot at the barasingh (Kashmir stag) which were still running in the forest; but, though I saw one fine one, the stalk proved impossible, and after lying for eight hours on the hillside, I had the satisfaction of seeing him disappear into the jungle. Eventually, as the first snow fell, about the middle of October, I determined that I had done enough for one season, and would set out at once for Bombay and home. Accordingly I started for Srinagar, which I reached on October 18th, having been away just five months. Here I made a short

A SUMMER IN HIGH ASIA.

but pleasant stay with Captain Godfrey, who was installed in the Residency, and, having packed up my trophies, which had been carefully preserved by one Mahadoo, skin-curer of Srinagar, and bid farewell to all the followers who had accompanied me in my rambles amongst the snowy peaks of Baltistan and stony plains of Thibet, I started down to Rawal Pindi. This part of my journey I accomplished in three days, doing the drive from Baramulla (over two hundred miles) in two days. Thence to Bombay, where I caught the good ship *Caledonia*, of the P. and O., whose first voyage it was, and made a passage home that easily broke the (then) record.

And thus ended my very pleasant ramble through "High Asia."

BUDDHIST PRAYER-WHEEL.

APPENDIX.

THE TRADE OF LADAKH WITH CHINA AND THIBET.

BY

CAPT. S. H. GODFREY

(LATE BRITISH JOINT COMMISSIONER OF LADAKH).

APPENDIX.

THE TRADE OF LADAKH WITH CHINA AND THIBET.

THE town of Leh is the great emporium of the trade which passes between India, Western China, and Thibet. The roads which lead from Russian Turkistan, Kashgaria and Yarkand, are joined by the Khutan caravan route, and meet in Leh. Lhassa, the sacred capital of Thibet, is connected with Ladakh by the trade route, which skirts the northern slopes of the Himalayas, and follows the valleys of the Brahmaputra and the Indus. These are the chief routes leading from foreign territory into Ladakh. Two roads diverge from Leh, linking up India with Asia. The Srinagar road leaves Leh in a westerly direction, and joins the Indian railway system at Rawal Pindi. The southern route, by the fertile Kullu Valley, runs down into two large commercial towns of India—Amritsar and Hushiarpur — and connects them with the markets of Central Asia.

Under a commercial Treaty concluded with the father of the present Maharajah of Kashmir, a British Commissioner is deputed to Ladakh to regulate and control the traders and the traffic, conjointly with an official appointed by the Kashmir State. These are the Joint Commissioners of Ladakh. The Kashmir official has to attend to the details of the interior administration of the province. The responsibility for the trade route practically devolves

A SUMMER IN HIGH ASIA.

upon the British Joint Commissioner, who resides in Leh during the trading season of each year, returning to India for the winter shortly before the passes are closed by snow. The pressure of foreign competition upon British commerce is felt even in these remote parts. Every market, however small, which is capable of development in British interests, is now a matter of concern. I shall therefore give a brief description of how the trans-Himalayan commerce of India is conducted in Leh, and attempt to show how far the Thibetan trade might, in expert opinion, be expanded and attracted to British markets.

The trade of Western Thibet and Chinese Turkistan is at present conducted in the following manner. Caravans, consisting chiefly of ponies and mules, make their annual start for Ladakh from the plains of the Punjab and the railway at Rawal Pindi in the summer. These carriers take up to Leh, by the Kullu and Kashmir routes, cotton goods, tea, and other merchandise, so timed that the convoy shall be delivered in Leh by the early autumn. Meanwhile the Central Asian traders will have set out from Lhassa, Khutan, Kashgar and Yarkand, to meet the Indian caravans at Leh, where both arrive in the autumn. Long-booted merchants of Russian Turkistan and the Chinese New Dominions exchange in the Leh markets, by barter and sale, their gold, silver and "charas," for the coral, cotton goods, and tea of the Indian traders. The Leh bazaar, thronged with men in the costume of many countries, and the native Ladakhi women, wearing their turquoise-studded peyrāks, forms a picturesque scene, whose bizarre effect is heightened by the Buddhist forms of architecture and ornamentation in the Rajah's palace, which overhangs the town. After a brief sojourn the strangers depart, east and west and south and north, before the great Himalayan passes are closed to traffic by the snow. The town then resumes the normal quiescence from which it has been temporarily aroused by the commerce. The alterations made in the road and the increase in the facilities for travelling, have lately induced the Central Asian merchants to pass through Leh and proceed to the Punjab to effect their purchases there, in the same way that the Siberian traders of to-day leave Nizhni-Novgorod, in Russia, to deal direct with St. Petersburg and Moscow. The great bulk of the business will continue for many years yet to be conducted after the old fashion in Ladakh, for changes take place very slowly in the East.

The trans-frontier trade through Leh has been steadily increasing since I assumed charge of the administration of the trade route as British Joint Commissioner of Ladakh. In 1893 the value of the trade rose from thirty-three lakhs of rupees to thirty-nine. The year I was in Ladakh it had reached sixty lakhs. A table will be found at the end of this chapter, which represents the value of the trade for the past ten years. It is clear that if the present rate of increase observable in the statistics of the past few years can be maintained, the trade of Thibet and Chinese Turkistan will become an important item in our Indian commerce. The existing system is capable of coping with a reasonable development of trade without increasing expenditure extravagantly, or incurring any political danger.

At first sight it would seem as though elaborate machinery would be necessary to preserve order in the Leh bazaars among the heterogeneous assemblage of polyglot merchants from Russia, India, China and Thibet. As a matter of fact trade disputes seldom occur, and, when they do, are generally settled by a system of arbitration in the serais. No caravan could get far from Leh without the necessary passport from the British Joint Commissioner. Eastward it would be stopped by the guard over the bridge at Khalsi, and northward in the Nubra Valley. Without supplies it would be helpless.

A SUMMER IN HIGH ASIA.

Only men of substance, too, visit the country for trading purposes. There is practically, therefore, no serious crime in the country. The Ladakhis are peace-loving and law-abiding, and no proletariat exists in the town. The Battery and Infantry Regiment of Kashmir troops which are quartered in the fort below the town of Leh, would be more than sufficient to overawe any mob that could collect in the wide bazaar, which is the principal market-place.

The system of road administration is curiously patriarchal. The trade route is maintained entirely at the expense of the Kashmir State, which under the treaty I have alluded to before, pays some few thousand rupees yearly to the Joint Commissioners for the upkeep of the road. The distance from the Zojila to the Karakoram is over three hundred miles. The distance from Leh to the Ladakh-Lahoul frontier is over a hundred. The total length of mountain road under the charge of the Joint Commissioners is not less than four hundred and fifty miles. The sum of a few hundred pounds would be manifestly inadequate for the maintenance of such a road over some of the highest passes in the world were it not for the assistance rendered to the Commissioners by the people of the country. On a call by the British Joint Commissioner the Ladakhis, who are practically dependent for their livelihood on the traffic and carrying trade of the country, will assemble immediately and work night and day to repair a broken bridge or road provided the British Joint Commissioner is present. At the conclusion of the work they willingly accept whatever remuneration the Commissioners may be able to vote to them out of the limited means placed at their disposal, and there is an end of the matter.

The problem of the further development of this trade centre is an interesting one. Russian competition may or may not drive British commerce out of Chinese Turkistan, as it has done in Asia Minor, in the north of Persia, in Central Asia, and threatens to do in the northern provinces

A SUMMER IN HIGH ASIA.

of China. In Thibet this competition has not yet been felt, and may yet be averted by securing the priority of entry. The trade of Lhassa with Ladakh and India seems capable of a large expansion. Captain Bower, in his interesting book, 'Across Thibet' (Chapter XVI., p. 282), says: "Amongst all classes—officials, Llamas, peasants, and nomads—a taste for trading is strongly developed, and all are ever ready to seize an opportunity for making money. The higher officials more particularly devote themselves to commerce, as the emoluments appertaining to their offices are exceedingly small, but the position gives them ample opportunities to trade with advantage, and these opportunities none fail to avail themselves of. The Llamas utilise portions of the great wealth their monasteries contain for trading purposes, the peasants nearly all devote a certain amount of attention to commerce, and the nomads are ever ready to dispose of wool and hides. As regards the prospects of trade with India should the country ever be open to commerce, of all articles in which we can hope to do a profitable trade, tea easily ranks first. At one time it was a Government monopoly, and even now I believe it is compulsorily sold to the people in some parts, the pressure being put on by members of the Government engaged in the trade. The population of Thibet, that is to say of Thibet proper, has been estimated at four millions. If they drank as much tea per head as is drunk in England, viz. five pounds, the annual consumption would be twenty million pounds, and even taking the consumption per head at the low figure of 3, that would give a total of twelve million pounds.

"Besides tea, other articles that would find a market, are sugar, tobacco, rice, crockery, tinted spectacles, red and yellow broadcloth, brass buttons, brightly stamped cotton cloth, and coral.

"Amongst the articles that Thibet can export, wool takes the foremost place. The capabilities of the country as regards the amount that could be supplied are practically unlimited. There is evidently a great accumulation of the precious metals in the country.

"The possibilities of Thibet as a future market are indisputable. The people would take tea and manufactured goods, and return raw material and the precious metals." So much for the tea trade. Captain Bower's views on the trade are practically confirmed by the opinion recorded in my last Trade Report from Leh, though this is expressed in more guarded and general terms. "With regard to the future, it will be no rash prediction to state that as long as the interest of the British Authority in it lasts, so long there will be every possibility of improvement in the trade; when this is withdrawn the trade will drop in proportion. The Residency has done what it can under the present conditions and with existing materials. The question of securing to the traders from our side equal rights in Chinese Turkistan with Russian subjects is one in which only the Government of India and the Pekin Embassy can move. Such security would undoubtedly add to the traffic, and from a purely commercial point of view would appear very desirable."

The method in which the upkeep of the trade route is managed has been explained. Some account of the manner in which the work is done may prove of interest. The adventures of my camp during the "flood-year" will illustrate this. Ladakh is shown in Ramsay's 'Western Thibetan Dictionary' as a rainless tract. In past years this was clearly the case. Increase of cultivation may be responsible for the climatic change. In the beginning of July a steady rain began in Kashmir and Ladakh, which worked havoc among the roads and bridges in both countries. The Indus, the Jhelum, and the rivers between Srinagar and Leh rose in flood, and communications between the two towns were completely cut off. The news of the destruction of the bridge at Kargil was telegraphed to me. By the time I had arrived there was no bridge left over the Sooroo, and the rivers which unite at Kargil were impassable. The place where the break had occurred was one hundred and twenty miles from the nearest town. Telegrams had to be despatched for wire and other material necessary, and the villagers were collected from the southern glens to fell the tall poplars at the Kargil fort, prepare planks, and forge rough nails which would be of use until supplies should arrive from Kashmir. The principal difficulty lay in the question of how to convey orders over a river across which the voice could not travel, and in which no boat or raft could hope to live. Ladakhis who had attempted to cross the river higher up had been drowned. The officers who were camped on the right bank of the river, unable to return to India, signalled that they were willing to do all in their power to help. A Ladakhi warrior was discovered who possessed a bow and arrow dating from the time when the country was ruled by its own Gyalpos or Kings. Orders summoning a road official from Leh were affixed to the shaft. It fell short and was lost. The next carried the message. By the same means plans and drawings were passed backwards and forwards. At this time the officers encamped opposite had a narrow escape. Their tents were pitched in some fields near the village of Chalaskot, beneath a range of snow-capped mountains towering many thousand feet precipitously above them. About midday a dull report was heard and a great piece of the mountain side appeared to be moving. A large area had become detached by the bursting of a subterranean lake, and was descending like a stream of lava upon the devoted camp. Work had fortunately been closed for the midday rest, so the camp was not deserted. Figures could be made out with the glasses striking the tents and moving horses and household goods and chattels. They were just in time. Everything

A SUMMER IN HIGH ASIA.

had been got out of the way as the mud stream swept past the village, carrying away trees, walls, fields and the very land on which the camp had stood down into the swollen and discoloured river. A lively exchange of arrows conveyed the assurance that all was well, and congratulations that the débâcle had not occurred at night.

On the completion of the bridge heads an iron arrow connected them by a fishing line. Along this a rope was passed, and the mails were put across. A telegraph wire was next placed in position, and within three weeks from this time a combined cantilever and suspension bridge, one span of which was one hundred and twenty-five feet across, was ready, to carry the traffic. The road was then diverted to pass along this route until the main bridge at Kargil should be reconstructed. The four broken bridges of the Lamayuru Nalah were next rebuilt, establishing free caravan communications with Leh.

The whole of the difficulties were not yet overcome. The Shyok River to the north of Leh on the further side of the Khardeny Pass was in full flood. The rafts had been wrecked and the caravans from Yarkand were blocked in the Nubra Valley. The Ladakhis and Baltis at Kargil and Leh stated that the trade was at a standstill for the present year at least.

My arrival at Leh caused a change in public opinion. The deputation which met the party below the town were assured that every endeavour would be made to re-open the road. Planks and material were hurried over the Khardong, a pass 17,500 feet high leading into the Shyok valley. The river at Sati was indeed found to be impracticable, but further down the valley there is a village where in former days a bridge was said to have existed, built in the time of a native governor of Ladakh, Mehtar Mangal. The remains of one pier are still visible. At this point two rafts were constructed, and an attempt made to connect the two banks by a hawser suspended from the high rocks on the right bank. The idea was that the rafts were to ply on the hawser. The experiment proved a dangerous one. The rapidly uncoiling ropes caught me by the foot while attending to the navigation of the first boat. I was thrown down immediately and dragged to the side of the raft. Happily the hawser parted at an unobserved flaw. Communications were, however, established, and three days afterwards the party had set out for the Karawul Dawan. All danger to the Central Asian trade was now over. The Karawul Dawan Pass is merely a steep hillside, very wearying to tired ponies, but never impassable. It might have been thought that the great altitude of the Sasser Pass, over 18,000 feet, would have rendered it impossible for regular traffic to cross it. This is not altogether so. The road is very rough, and marvellous wastes of ice and snow meet on the Sasser glacier. They present those difficulties to the traveller on the Pass, which must be inherent in the Arctic desolation of the place, where there is no sign of human habitation except the little stone huts of the goat-herds who pasture their flocks below the Pass in summer. The rise to the glacier is gradual, crossing a moraine where patches of grass in July are studded with edelweiss and Alpine flowers. The glacier itself is a broad sheet of ice deeply covered with hard frozen snow and shut in on either hand by splintered crags glistening with snow and ice. The eternal silence is only broken by the passage of the caravans. Provided that the road is not blocked by fallen fragments of ice, the negotiation of the Sasser is less wearying to animals than the ascent of the comparatively low Zojila.

Here the work of my party ceased. They might well claim to have done yeoman's service for the Empire. Within two months a broken mountain road of two hundred miles, crossing three large rivers and three passes of over 17,000 feet, had been put into a condition to carry the Central Asian trade without further hitch and was in thorough order from end to end. The officers who had started with me, simply to shoot and travel, and had remained with me throughout the whole of our difficult and trying task, were thanked in the name of the State by the Kashmir Wazir Wazarat, who gave a dinner in their honour at Leh on their safe return and on the reopening of the Central Asian road.

Much has been written lately about the necessity for pushing British trade. Many appear to be of opinion that it should be left to private enterprise to extend our commerce. In Central Asia it is impossible for private enterprise to succeed unless the State can show that the road is open and the markets are not closed by foreign fiscal regulations. When diplomatic action has secured the right of entry for our merchandise into Thibet on conditions not less favourable than those accorded to other countries, and Indian merchants are allowed to pass freely to and fro in the southern and western provinces of the Chinese Empire, the Thibetan markets should provide no inconsiderable outlet for British manufactures and the products of our Indian Empire. The Indian Government do not appear to view with disfavour the prospect of an increase in our trans-Himalayan trade, but a certain amount of active support is necessary if its development is to proceed as satisfactorily as might be desired. If a small portion only of the large frontier military expenditure could be diverted to a more peaceful purpose, it would bring a livelihood, if not wealth, to many, and enable the nomad Thibetans to dispose of produce which is useless to them unless they can sell their surplus or exchange it for the produce of more favoured climates or more civilised countries. The Government which shall accomplish this will have done a public service greater than the acquisition of districts whose revenue cannot pay the cost of administration. No policy of aggression or annexation is desirable, nor would it be profitable to the

A SUMMER IN HIGH ASIA.

SCHEDULE OF THE TRADE STATISTICS SHOWN BY THE BRITISH JOINT COMMISSIONER'S OFFICE AT LADAKH.

Year.	Import.	Export.	Total.
	Rs.	Rs.	Rs.
1885	1,831,501	1,569,321	3,400,822
1886-87 . . .	1,652,413	1,232,229	2,884,642
1887-88 . . .	1,716,245	1,712,328	3,428,573
1888-89 . . .	1,353,845	1,212,030	2,565,875
1889-90 . . .	1,600,580	1,513,626	3,114,206
1890-91 . . .	1,525,483	1,440,906	2,966,389
1891-92 . . .	1,565,278	1,447,840	3,013,118
1892-93 . . .	1,795,141	1,591,544	3,386,685
1893-94 . . .	2,154,252	1,837,375	3,991,627
1894-95 . . .	3,165,218	2,850,101	6,015,321
Total . . .	18,359,956	16,407,301	33,766,258
Average . . .	1,835,995	1,640,730	3,376,625

SCHEDULE OF THE STATISTICS OF TRADE BETWEEN INDIA, TURKISTAN, AND THIBET, FROM THE OFFICE OF THE BRITISH JOINT COMMISSIONER AT LADAKH.

Year.		India.	Turkistan.	Chang Thang.	Total.
		Rs.	Rs.	Rs.	Rs.
Imports from	1893-94 .	1,284,162	757,112	112,978	2,154,252
	1894-95 .	1,731,680	1,274,700	158,837	3,165,218
Exports from	1893-94 .	763,837	1,017,029	56,509	1,837,375
	1894-95 .	1,314,143	1,440,599	95,360	2,850,102

end in view. The road into Thibet should be opened to native traders of India, and they should be allowed to compete on equal terms with all comers along a highway free and open to all. In the opinion of men qualified to judge, our trans-Himalayan trade would then rapidly assume proportions which would attract more general attention than it receives at present, and would develop a most useful and profitable market for both Great Britain and India.

The suggestion to increase the expenditure on the Ladakh office seems to be a question which should be discussed and decided on its merits, with a view to ascertaining whether or no any public benefit, or the reverse, might accrue if the proposal were to meet with approval. Perhaps the best means of explaining this will be, while abstaining from personal opinion, to make a plain statement of fact of what occurred in Ladakh in 1894, and the measures taken to meet the emergency, and then contrast the results obtained with what would have happened had those measures not been taken.

On or about July 5th, while awaiting the orders of the Government of India, at Gulmarg, on certain proposals contained in the Ladakh Trade Report of 1893-94, I received a telegram that postal and all other communications from Leh and Central Asia had been completely cut off by the destruction of the Kargil bridge. The telegraph line is only laid as far as Kargil on the Leh road, so that nothing could be ascertained of what had happened beyond Kargil.

The Ladakh diary will show that on July 6th I left Gulmarg, and, proceeding by double marches, reached Kargil on the 10th. On arrival there I found that not only were no traces of the Kargil bridge, except the remnants of the two end piers, left, but every bridge on the Sooroo had been destroyed by the floods, and there was absolutely no means of communicating with the right

A SUMMER IN HIGH ASIA.

bank. Fifteen miles up the Sooroo I found Colonel Ward vainly endeavouring to get the Baltis, at Chalaskat, to bring in material to try and bridge the river there. The fact is alluded to to show that the presence of the British Joint Commissioner on the spot is absolutely necessary on a crisis of this description occurring. The villagers at that time stated that bridges could only be built at low water in winter, and that it was hopeless to try and place timber in position over an impassable river from one bank only, especially as the central pier had gone. Such materials as were available at Kargil, and several hundred labourers, were collected at once. Two days afterwards an urgent message was shot over the river, wrapped round the shaft of an arrow, empowering two officers, delayed on the opposite bank, to take any requisite measures to compel the inhabitants to work, and a second was sent to summon the road darogha from Ladakh. The roar of the river prevented verbal communication, but a heavy-headed arrow took a fishing-line across, and so connected the pier-heads now under construction. Along this a double rope, capable of carrying a manual weight across the river, was formed into an endless chain at the bridge heads, and the mails were safely passed from side to side. I now knew the extent of the damage done, and that every day was of the greatest importance. The inhabitants worked with a will, the whole of my Staff and several officers with my camp being busy from daybreak to dark.

On July 23rd the cantilevers were successfully connected, and I crossed on the two poles to place in position the third on which the strength and utility of the structure depended. Next day this was got over, and an officer, who had been detained on the right bank, proceeded down to India. On July 26th the bridge was opened to the traffic awaiting its completion on both banks. Two photographs of the Sooroo bridge are attached. The central span is one hundred

A SUMMER IN HIGH ASIA.

and twenty-five feet between perpendiculars. The photographs give little idea of the pace and volume of the water, which were the chief causes of the difficulties. The importance of the work to the Central Asian trade was evinced by the fact that every merchant delayed at Chalaskat worked without remuneration, as a coolie, many of these merchants being men of very considerable wealth and position. The smaller bridges caused little delay, the new structure over the Indus having fortunately withstood the flood. I therefore reached Leh on August 3rd. Here I heard that the rafts on the Shyok at Sati, on the north of Leh, had been washed down the river and wrecked, and that the caravans, which had arrived on the right bank, were blocked there. The planks, ordered the previous year, were therefore hurried over the Khardang Pass, and on August 11 I was in camp by the side of the Shyok river. The Ladakh diaries of that and succeeding days will show that on the 13th one of the rafts was moving, and that my camp had moved up to the Karawul Dawan and Sasser passes to restore broken communication there, and that I was in camp till August 27th. By this time the Khardang Pass and valley, the Shyok rafts and road, the Nubra Valley, and Karawul Dawan and Sasser passes had been put into a passable condition for regular pack traffic, and all danger to the through traffic was over.

During these moves I paid for all transport at full rates as far as my personal camp and baggage were concerned, only Durbar engineering stores and material being carried at cheap rates, in agreement with the villagers, whose income from the transport of the trade absolutely depended on the re-opening of the road, and who gave some months work practically gratis. For the camp at the Sooroo Colonel Barr allowed ten days halting allowance to my office establishment on the understanding that I would not ask for it myself. This

SOOROO BRIDGE, UNDER CONSTRUCTION.

A SUMMER IN HIGH ASIA.

I volunteered myself in order to prevent that small concession being refused to men who had done more than their ordinary work and been put to heavy expense when camped at fifteen miles away from the nearest village on the barren bank of a river where wood and water only were locally procurable. In the Nubra and beyond I took no one I could do without, and so reduced office expenses; but the travelling allowance given, Rs. 110 per mensem or Rs. 4 per diem roughly, did not cover cost of transport alone, and could not have come well within Rs. 100 per mensem of what was spent by me privately in connection with my movements? But it will not, I think, be difficult to understand that I had little time for private accounts. At Chalaskat a merchant's caravan of stores had to be bought up to keep the camp going. In the Nubra stores had to be sent out from Leh. Nothing could have saved the communications in 1894 had not the year before a road been run under my supervision along the right bank of the Shergol gorge. Of the eight bridges by which the old road passed backwards and forwards in 1892 no traces of seven had been left by the floods of 1894. That was the main work of those years. After my return from Nubra in August of that year, I had to make several tours to watch work under construction. Without the superintendence of some one with some slight knowledge of engineering, this work could not possibly have been completed in time. It is needless to say that more than the travelling allowance of Rs. 110 per mensem had been spent long before the Nubra was reached, apart from the cost of the wear and tear of property involved by long and rapid moves over a broken line of communications. The distance from Srinagar to Leh being 250 miles, from Leh to the Sasser 110, I had to travel over 700 miles, exclusive of occasional flying visits of thirty to fifty miles a day.

A SUMMER IN HIGH ASIA.

In 1894 alone the following major works were completed. The Sooroo bridge, of which a photograph is given. The figures on the bridge will show on a rough scale the size of the work which had to be completed in a limited space of time.

The new Kargil bridge, a more solid and considerably larger structure than that over the Sooroo, was constructed later.

The main bridge over the Indus was designed, aligned and begun in 1893, but completed by the early summer of 1894.

The Kardang pass and road.

The new rafts in the Shyok and the Koyak ferry.

The Karawul Dawan approach and pass.

The Sasser pass and road and shelters on the last two passes.

These works were in hand at these points simultaneously, and had to be inspected occasionally.

The whole was completed without the expenditure of any of the Government of India money on the works. The extra expenditure incurred by me in connection with my camp was paid by me. The head men of the country were mostly rewarded by seats in Durbar and my written thanks. We might now consider what would have been the result of the non-completion of any of the main works, the bridge at the Sooroo, that over the Indus, or the rafts of the Shyok river. Had the first not been constructed, the whole of the India caravans would have been blocked at Kargil. Unable to obtain provisions or transport from that half of Kargil town and the villages which lie on the right bank of the river, these caravans must have returned to Kashmir for the winter, for we knew when postal communication had been re-established that the country north of Leh was impassable. Had I remained at Leh instead of continuing my journey towards Central Asia, the Yarkand caravans would have had to return from the Shyok before winter overtook

SOOROO BRIDGE, COMPLETED.

CALIFORNIA

A SUMMER IN HIGH ASIA.

them, since the Nubra valley alone could not have supported them. The trade, therefore, which had risen from thirty-three to thirty-nine lakhs in 1893, in 1894, instead of again rising to sixty lakhs, would have fallen to something not far removed from nil, and the growing reputation of the Ladakh trade route would have suffered a blow from which it would not easily have recovered.

It appears from this that the British Joint Commissioner must be on the move on an emergency arising. And at present, it is a fact that he cannot do this without spending private money. Such floods as those of 1894 may possibly, of course, not recur for years to come, and the main bridges now finished will probably stand for many years. But any heavy break, even in the road, will still have serious effects if not promptly put right. It is not only in the year under note that heavy work had to be, and was, done.

I have written this note at perhaps tedious length, because the Government of India will naturally not at present agree to any increase of expenditure without good reason being shown, and in order to demonstrate that this increase is necessary, *if it be an object to secure and increase the Central Asian trade.* The expenditure proposed amounts to some hundreds of rupees per annum only, while the trade is worth some lakhs.

The question merits full consideration whether this trade cannot be developed to an extent which will benefit more than local commerce despite what I have said above. If, therefore, I may offer an opinion which seems unbiassed and which is based on some three years' experience of Ladakh, I would suggest that the question of whether it is not worth while to incur a small definite expenditure to secure a not inconsiderable influx and efflux of commerce from and to India is a matter which would seem to merit full consideration.

S. H. GODFREY.

A SUMMER IN HIGH ASIA.

NOTE ON TRADE BETWEEN INDIA AND LADAKH.

[NOTE. Official figures for the trade of Ladakh with the neighbouring states other than India are not obtainable in this country for a later date than 1895. As we may now expect to have more intimate relations than heretofore with Thibet, and a marked improvement in the whole trans-frontier traffic, it might be advantageous to British merchants to have the detailed reports of the Commissioners in the Frontier-States transmitted regularly from Simla. The following table, taken from the latest 'India Land Trade Accounts,' brings the statistics for Ladakh up to the 31st of March, 1898 (pp. 210-211):—

	1895-6.	1896-7.	1897-8.
Imports (rupees)	421,633	571,880	526,616
Exports ,,	393,578	580,853	467,248
Total	815,211	1,152,733	933,864
(15 Rs. = £1)	£54,347	£74,849	£62,257

Neither the exportation nor the importation of treasure is included in these figures. According to the 'Statistical Abstract' (1897), the treasure-account stands as follows for the years mentioned (p. 218):—

	1895-6.	1896-7.
Imports (tens of rupees)	960	320
Exports ,, ,,	4,226	6,500
Total	5,186	6,820

A SUMMER IN HIGH ASIA.

In his 'Review of the Trade of India for 1897-8' (p. 69), Mr. T. A. Robertson takes the first table substantially as it stands, though he expresses his results in tens of rupees. He makes the following comments on the general trade-situation:

"The trade with countries across the Indian Frontier remained practically stationary. The trade with Kabul and Kandahar is dwindling owing to the fiscal restrictions placed upon it by the Amir, and last year further contraction was caused by the closing of the Khyber Pass and the military operations on the frontier. The effect of the fighting in the Swat is noticeable in a set-back to the expanding trade of Bajaur, while the requisition for the frontier campaign of all available transport affected the trade of Kashmir and Ladakh. The most important trade on the frontier is with Nepal, and this shows a marked increase, as does also the trade with Thibet" (p. 4).

T. B. B.]

CURIOS FROM LEH.

LIST OF BUTTERFLIES FROM THIBET.

LIST OF BUTTERFLIES FROM THIBET.

2	*Danais chrysippus*, Linnæus	Very common.
35	*Œneis pumilus*, Felder	Good.
3	*Amecera schakra*, Kollar	,,
3	*Epinephile roxane*, Felder	,,
4	,, *sp.* (not named in M. Collection)	,,
3	*Hipparchia swaha*, Kollar	Common.
2	,, *parisatis*, Kollar	,,
1	*Argynnis childreni*, Gray	Not common.
18	,, *jainadeva*, Moore	Very common.
7	*Melitæa minerva*, Staudinger	Very good.
1	*Vanessa charonia*, Drury	Not rare.
3	,, *polychloros*, Linnæus	Good.
4	,, *cashmirensis*, Kollar	,,
6	,, *ladakensis*, Moore	,,
4	,, *agnicula*, Moore	,,
1	*Pyrameis callirhoë*, Millière	,,
5	,, *cardui*, Linnæus	Common.
1	*Sibythea lepita*, Moore	,,
9	*Chrysophanus timeus*, Cramer	,,
6	,, *turcicus*, Girhard	,,
2	*Polyommatus bæticus*, Linnæus	,,
13	*Plebius pheretes*, Hubner	Fairly good.
9	*Cupido ariana*, Moore	Common.
6	*Synchloe callidice*, Esper (1 ♂)	Good.
4	,, *chloridice*, Hubner	Fairly good.
9	,, *daplidice*, Linnæus	Common.
6	*Ganoris rapæ*, Linnæus	,,
7	,, *brassicæ*, Linnæus	,,

A SUMMER IN HIGH ASIA.

4	*Ganoris gliciria*, Cramer	Fairly good.
1	„ *krueperi*, Staudinger	Very good.
4	*Gonepteryx rhammi*, Linnæus	Common.
20	*Colias edusina*, Felder	„
10	„ *pallida*, Staudinger	Fairly good.
19	„ *sareptensis*, Staudinger	„
12	„ *ladakensis*, Felder	Rare.
2	„ *glacialis*, McLachlan	„
2	*Parnassius epaphus*, Uberthür	„
1	„ *acco*, Gray	„
1	„ *charltonius*, Gray	„
9	*Papilio machaon*, Linnæus	Common.
1	*Cyaniris kasmira*, Moore	„
2	*Colias erate*, Esper	Good.

MOTHS.

1	*Hypercompa principalis*, Kollar	Common.
3	*Heliothis dipsacea*, Linnæus	„

NOTE.—Specimens of each of these butterflies were presented to the Natural History Museum, and are now at South Kensington.

INDEX.

ANTELOPE, 172, 182.

"BADMINTON LIBRARY" on nyan, 135.
Baltal, red bear, 11; ibex, 12; barasingh, 250.
Barasingh, 250.
Bear, 3, 10, 11, 16, 18, 21, 22.
Birds (unnamed), 45, 94, 131.
Bower on nāpoo, 136; goa, 172; Chinese Thibet, 182.
Burhel. *See* Nāpoo.
Butterflies (unnamed), 132; *Papilio machaon*, 100; *Vanessa Ladakensis*, 210. *See* List, 281, 282.
Buzzard, 189.

CATERPILLAR plague in Kashmir, 8, 9.
Chiff-chaff, 46.
Chorbat-La, ibex, 87, 88; marmots, 91; birds (unnamed), 94.
Chough, 131.
"Churten," description of, 100, 101.
Cricket, 215.
Currant-moth (*Abraxas grossulariata*), 9.

DOG (wild), 120.
Dongan, snipe, 210; neighbourhood, of goa, 210, 211; kyang, 210, 211.
Doomkhar, nalah, ibex, 103.
Do-oo, neighbourhood of, ibex, 84.
Drew on mountain sickness, 92, 93.
Duck, 189, 209; *Casarca rutila*, 175, 221.

FISH (unnamed), 191, 209.
Fox (*Vulpes ferrilatus*), 221.

"GALLERY," description of, 30, 33.
Gazelle. *See* Goa.

283

INDEX.

Gelinot (Snow-lark), 131.
Goa, 162, 163, 166, 169–172, 176, 179, 185, 193, 201–212, 222, 223, 231.
Goma Hanoo, neighbourhood of, ibex, 97 ; snow-leopard, 98.
Goond, neighbourhood of, black bear, 10.
Goose, 221 ; *Anser indicus*, 175, 189, 217.
Grouse, 212, 215.
Gull, 175.
Gya Nalah (Kayma, Tubbuh), birds (unnamed), snow-pigeons, Ram Chukore, ravens, choughs, gelinots, vultures, lammergeiers, hawks, Ladakhi marmots, hares, 131 ; butterflies (unnamed), 132 ; nāpoo, 132, 139, 145–149 ; nÿan, 132, 139, 140–142 : wolf, 146.

"HALLAL," 73, 206.
Hanlé, neighbourhood of, kyang, 188, 193, 200, 202 ; mosquitoes, 188, 189 ; buzzard, goose (*Anser indicus*), pigeons, hares, duck, 189 ; fish (unnamed), 191 ; nÿan, 193–200 ; nāpoo, 193, 201 ; wolf, 199 ; goa, 193, 202–206.
Hare, 46, 131, 145, 189.
Hawk, 131.
Hoopoe, 46.
Hushe, main and side nalahs, ibex, 19, 34, 37, 46, 52, 56, 59, 65–68, 71–74, 77–80 ; oorin, 52–55.

IBEX, 6, 11, 12, 15, 19, 22, 24, 25, 27, 34, 37, 46, 48, 49, 51, 52, 56–80, 84, 86–88, 91, 93, 97, 103, 104, 106, 108, 119, 228, 237, 242, 244.

"JHULA" BRIDGE, description of, 35–37.

KAPALU, neighbourhood of, hares, partridge, 46.
Kayma. *See* Gya Nalah.
Kharbu, mountains near, ibex, 242.
Kiameri-La, neighbourhood of, nÿan, 150 151 ; wolf, 151.
Kinlock on nÿan, 132, 133.
Kiris, birds (unnamed), magpies, 45 ; hoopoes, orioles, ravens, chiff-chaffs, 46.
Koyul, nÿan, 201, 209.
Kustang, neighbourhood of, Ladakhi marmots, 85 ; Ram Chukore, shāpoo, ibex, 86.
Kyang (*Equus hemionus*), 150, 162–164, 169, 175, 179, 188, 193, 200, 202, 210, 211.

Lagomys Ladakensis (Ladakh Pika, Sterndale), 165.
Lam Tso. *See* Dongan, neighbourhood of.
Lammergeier, 131, 222.

INDEX.

Lanak-La, neighbourhood of, fish (unnamed), 209; *Vanessa Ladakensis*, 210; lizard, locust (cricket), 215.
Leopard (*Felis uncia*), 98, 120.
Lizard, 215.
Locust, 215.
Lynx, 215; (*Felis Isabellinus*), Ee, 180.

MACINTYRE on mountain sickness, 92; on nÿan, 133.
Magpie, 30, 45.
"Mani" stone, description of, 100.
Marmot (*Arctomys caudatus*), 16, 246; *Arctomys aureus*, 85, 91, 131.
Mataiyan Valley, Kashmiri marmot, 246.
Miru Nalah, side ravine, shāpoo, 225-228.
Mitsahoï, neighbourhood of, Kashmiri marmots, 16.
Moorcroft on mountain sickness, 177.
Mosquito, 40, 188, 189.
Mountain sickness, 81, 92-94, 156-158, 176, 177.
"Mountaineer" on nÿan, 133.

NĀPOO, Burhel (*Ovis nahura*), 119-121, 126, 132, 135-139, 142-150, 180, 193, 194, 201, 209, 218, 222, 223, 228, 238.
Nÿan (*Ovis Ammon, Ovis Hodgsoni*), 75, 113, 121, 126, 132-142, 145, 150, 151, 162, 163, 169, 171, 175-177, 181, 182, 191-201, 204, 209, 217, 218, 223, 231.

OORIN. *See* Shāpoo.
Ooti, goa, 212; sand-grouse, 212, 215; lynx, 215.
Oriole, 30, 46.
Ovis Ammon. *See* Nÿan.
Ovis Hodgsoni. *See* Nÿan.
Ovis nahura. *See* Nāpoo.
Ovis Polii, 108, 135.
Ovis vignei. *See* Shāpoo.

PANDRAS, neighbourhood of, red bear, 18, 21, 22.
Papilio machaon, 100.
"Parri," description of, 29, 32.
Partridge ("chikore"), 46, 48, 49.
Peldo Le, goose (*Anser indicus*), 217.
Pigeon, 51, 131, 145, 189.
Polakonka-La, nÿan, 176, 177; kyang, 179.
Poongook, teal, duck, nāpoo, 209
Puga, nāpoo, 180.
Puttatuktuk, goa, 170, 171, 176.

INDEX.

RAM Chukore, Snow-cock (*Tetraogallus Himalayensis*), 86, 131.
Raven, 46, 131.

SHĀPOO, Oorin (*Ovis vignei*), 52–55, 86, 104, 105, 139, 206, 224–228, 237, 241, 242, 244.
Sheep (four-horned), 108.
Snipe, 128, 198, 210.
Snow-cock. *See* Ram Chukore.
Snow-lark (Gelinot), 131.
Snow-leopard, 98, 120.
Swallow tail (*Papilio machaon*), 100.

TAGALANG-LA, lammergeier, 222.
Tahr, 74.
Tashgaum, neighbourhood of, ibex, 24, 25, 91.
Teal, 209.
Tern, 175.
Tiri Nalah, table-land near, nẏan, 162, 169; kyang, 162; Ladakh Pika, 165; goa, 169.
Tolti; mosquitoes, 40.
Tso-Kar (*See* also Puttatuktuk), wolf, 166, 169; goa, 169; kyang, 169, 175; duck (*Casarca rutila*), 175, 221; goose (*Anser indicus*), 175, 221; tern, gull, 175; nẏan, 175, 176; wolf, 175, 176; Thibetan fox, 221.
Tubbuh. *See* Gya Nalah.

Vanessa Ladakensis, 210.
Vulture, 131, 222.

WAKHA NALAH, ibex, 242.
Ward on nẏan, 133, 141, 203, 204.
Wolf, 120, 146, 147, 151, 166, 169, 175, 176, 199.

YĀK (wild), 172, 181, 182.
Yogma Hanoo, neighbourhood of, *Papilio machaon*, 100.

ZĀK, description of, 42–44.
Zogi-La, ibex, 15.

www.ingramcontent.com/pod-product-compliance
Lightning Source LLC
Chambersburg PA
CBHW031328230426
43670CB00006B/270